The Matchless Vale

THE STORY OF HAM AND PETERSHAM AND THEIR PEOPLE

Written and compiled by Vanessa Fison

Design, photography and production by Alison Graham

Edited by David Yates

First Published in 2009
Reprinted with amendments 2018

© Ham and Petersham Association, 2009

ISBN 978-0-9563244-0-5

British Library Cataloguing in Publication Data
A catalogue record for this book is available from the British Library

Design, photography and production by
The London Design Factory
020 8332 2432

Printed by Imago Publishing Ltd

'Slow let us trace the matchless Vale of Thames...' The Seasons by James Thomson, 1727

Acknowledgements

Much of the information in the book has been drawn from the Journals of the Richmond Local History Society and the Local Studies Library in Richmond, and I am very grateful to both organisations.

I would like to record the help and encouragement I have received from many local residents, particularly Sylvia Peile, Martin Rice Edwards, Len Chave, Lilias Grey Turner, Jackie Latham, Frances Cave, and Celia Nelson. Particular thanks are due to John Cloake who pointed me in the right direction and who has drawn attention to a number of matters and made important corrections to the text.

My special thanks go to Alison Graham of the London Design Factory. She spent many hours with her camera around Ham and Petersham searching for blue skies throughout two grey summers. Without her skill and expertise in matters of design and production, this project would not have been possible.

Finally, but not least, to David Yates who has not only offered unstinting advice and encouragement but has also painstakingly edited the text.

A note about the Ham and Petersham Association. Its origins date from as early as 1933, when it was known as the Ham Ratepayers' Association. It then became the Ham and Petersham Ratepayers' and Residents' Association and in 1989 the name finally became the less cumbersome Ham and Petersham Association. In this book, I have generally referred to it by its current title. Throughout its long history the Association has been an integral part of the community, and it is essentially because of public-spirited members who over the years have voluntarily contributed their effort and time to seek to protect the unique environment of Ham and Petersham that it remains so special today. It is to all those people that this book is dedicated.

Vanessa Fison
May, 2009

Ham

For Ham locations see detailed map on pages 12 and 13.

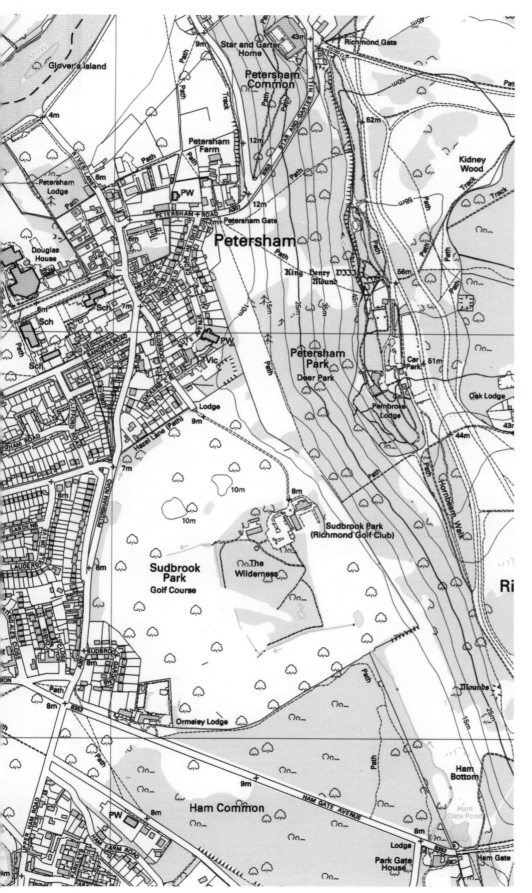

Petersham

For Petersham locations see detailed map on pages 72 and 73.

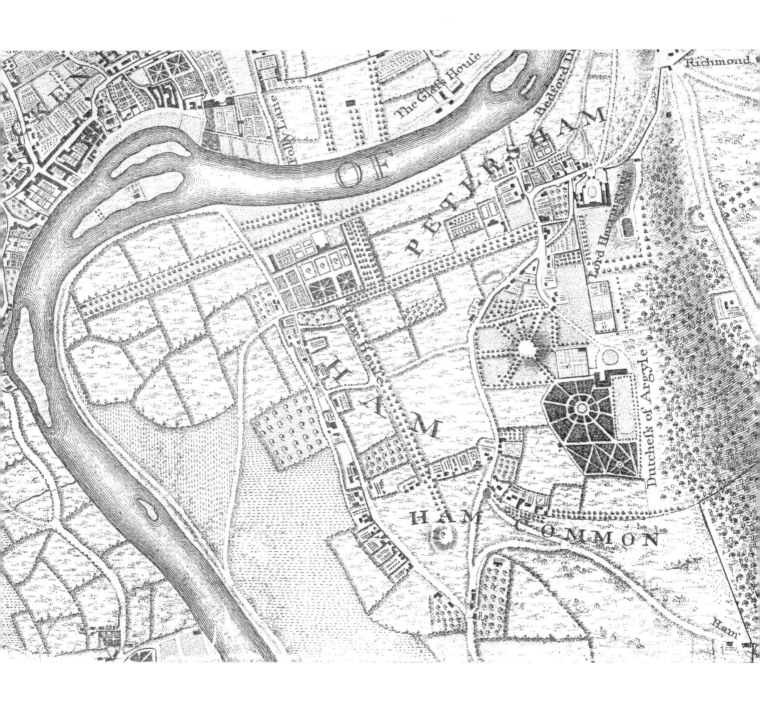

John Rocque's map of Ham and Petersham c.1746
Reproduced by kind permission of the
Local Studies Library, Richmond

Introduction

Ham and Petersham are a neighbouring pair of ancient villages on the south bank of the river Thames which, to a remarkable extent, have managed to preserve their village status and historical character in spite of the developmental pressures of the 19th and 20th centuries. The aim of this book is to celebrate what makes the two villages so special and of such interest by bringing together a selection of the available relevant historical material both in words and in pictures. It pays particular attention to the buildings and the people who lived and worked in them, but does not aim to be comprehensive; often only an outline can be given if the account is to remain within reasonable bounds.

The village of Petersham was recorded in the Domesday Book of 1086 as *Patricesham*, on land owned by Chertsey Abbey. The survey mentions a church, which would have been St Peter's, and a fishery 'worth 1,000 eels and 1,000 lampreys'. It is thought the village of Ham derived its name from *Hamme*, an old English word meaning meadowland in a bend of a river. It was a hamlet of Kingston, and until 1897 was known as Ham with Hatch.

Originally, Ham was the village along Ham Street and the land to the west of it in the river bend, together with a large part of what is now Richmond Park stretching east as far as the Robin Hood Gate. Hatch was a small area on the north side of Ham Common (the open part of which was at one time called Hatch Green). Hatch was a part of the Manor of Kingston Canbury which had belonged to Merton Priory, and did not come into the same ownership as Ham until the Canbury manor was bought by Wilbraham Tollemache, 6th Earl of Dysart, in the late 18th century. The manor of Ham, originally part of Kingston, was purchased by

King Henry V in 1415. At the same time he acquired Petersham manor from Chertsey Abbey in exchange for lands elsewhere.

In the 15th and 16th centuries Ham and Petersham were royal manors leased to the Cole family (see page 78). In the 17th century the lease passed to William Murray, 1st Earl of Dysart, of Ham House, and in 1671 the Duke of Lauderdale, who had married William's daughter Elizabeth Murray as her second husband, secured the lands of Ham and Petersham in freehold for the Lord of the Manor from the Crown.

Charles I's determination to enclose Richmond New Park in 1637 faced some considerable opposition, not only from his advisors but also from the landowners whose lands were affected. Traditional rights of way would be blocked to ordinary citizens, and the further taxes that would be required to fund New Park would make the King even more unpopular than he already was. Despite this opposition Charles was determined to press ahead with a hunting park for his private use. A number of neighbouring landowners around the Park were prevailed upon to part with their land, and the terms were generous. Both private and common land in Ham (895 acres) and, to a lesser extent, in Petersham (306 acres) were enclosed to form the Park. In return Charles entered into a Deed of Gift in 1635, granting £4,000 to the two villages and the commons not enclosed to the inhabitants in perpetuity. As commoners they had rights to graze and water their livestock and collect firewood. Charles built nearly ten miles of high wall around the perimeter of the 2,500 acres of his Great Park. Perhaps we should be grateful to the King; without his initiative much of the open space both on the Common and within the Park would by now have been claimed for development.

The history of both Ham and Petersham from the 17th century onwards is inextricably linked to the Lords of the Manor, the Dysarts of Ham House. They owned most of the land and were a strong influence on the form and historic development of both villages. The 17th and 18th centuries were a golden age for Ham and Petersham: they became a fashionable country retreat for the aristocracy and many of the elegant mansions built at that time still survive. Of the two, Ham was the more agricultural village, there being three large farms all owned by the Dysarts and these were worked by tenant farmers. The rich floodplains by the river provided fertile ground for both grazing and arable farming and later also for fruit and flower cultivation in market gardens.

Petersham provides the foreground of the famous view from Richmond Hill, across the Petersham Meadows, with Ham beyond. Unlike Kingston and Richmond, Ham and Petersham were never reached by the railways and that, together with the fact that there was no bridge which connected them to Twickenham on the other side of the river, was one of the reasons they escaped the rapid building expansion that took place during the Victorian period.

The early 20th century was a time of great change, particularly for Ham: agriculture was in decline and the Dysarts were aware of the possibilities of large-scale housing development at a time of growing population. However, there was a fear that development would harm the view from Richmond Hill, and there were similar fears regarding the lands on the Twickenham side of the Thames. The famous View, so celebrated by artists and poets, was also central to the fortunes of the town of Richmond, reliant as it was upon its rural attractions. Agreement was reached between landowners with the passing of the 1902 Richmond, Petersham and Ham Open Spaces Act. The Dysarts agreed to give up Petersham Meadows and Petersham Common to the Richmond Corporation for use as designated Open Space for public use; Ham Common was to be vested in the Ham District Council and in return Lammas Rights, (concerning grazing, see page 33), were extinguished over 176 acres of Ham Fields. Building did not start immediately though: instead the Dysarts leased the area to the Ham River Grit Company for the profitable working of gravel pits.

Above: a view from Richmond Hill towards Ham and Petersham c.1720 by Leonard Knyff. At 77 x 183 cm it is one of the largest panoramas ever to be painted in England

Below: the same view today

Up to the 18th century local government in Ham and Petersham was primarily a matter for the manorial courts. Both manors had their 'courts baron', as did Richmond; but the 'court leet' in Richmond from 1626 had jurisdiction also over Ham and Petersham. It appointed the manorial officials and could deal with matters somewhat more serious than the affairs of the court baron but not grave enough for the magistrates or the crown courts. In the 18th century the parish vestries began to have more importance, especially in the administration of the Poor Laws, and by the end of that century had largely superseded the manorial courts as the effective instruments of local government. Although Ham did not have its own parish church until St Andrew's was built in 1831, it had separate parochial status and its own vestry from the middle of the 17th century.

In 1892 Petersham was incorporated into the Borough of Richmond. In 1858 under the provisions of the Local Government Act of that year, the Ham Common Local Government District was formed and governed by a local board of eight members. In 1894 a further Local Government Act reconstituted the area as Ham Urban District, with an elected council of ten members replacing the local board. In 1933 Ham was divided up between the boroughs of Richmond and Kingston, the major share going to Richmond. Richmond combined Ham and Petersham into a new Sudbrook Ward. It was not until 1965 that the Ham and Petersham wards were established. During the 1930s large-scale residential development started to take place in Ham and it became a target for Council development as well as private housing which continued well into the 1960s.

The 9th Earl of Dysart died in 1935 with no direct heirs; he was the last Earl of Dysart to live at Ham House. The Dysart estate at this time was in decline. The Second World War also took its toll. Ham House and its gardens were donated to the National Trust in 1948, and in 1949 the Dysart family took the momentous step of selling approximately 350 acres of their remaining Ham and Petersham estate by auction, including 41 residences and 99 cottages. Much of the land went for development.

Sadly, many of the Dysart estate papers were destroyed or damaged when Sir Lyonel Tollemache (a distant cousin of the 9th Earl who had inherited Ham House) deposited all the Dysart deeds and papers in safe deposits at Chancery Lane for safe-keeping in the 1939–45 war. No doubt it was thought that the Hawker aircraft factory near to Ham House (then temporarily

By Order of the Buckminster Estates.

SURREY

In the Parishes of

HAM AND PETERSHAM

Particulars, Plans and Conditions of Sale

of the FREEHOLD of the

HAM AND PETERSHAM ESTATE

comprising

41 RESIDENCES

(many of which are period houses of historical interest) subject to existing tenancies, with
CONSIDERABLE REVERSIONARY VALUES

A FARM   TWO MODERN LICENSED PREMISES
FOUR SHOPS   A RIFLE RANGE
A GRAVEL AND SAND WORKS
NINETY-NINE COTTAGES   SUNDRY ALLOTMENTS
A PARCEL OF FREEHOLD GROUND RENTS
and a number of Plots suitable for Building

The whole extending to about

350 Acres

To be Sold by Auction, in Lots (unless previously sold by Private Treaty), by

DEBENHAM, TEWSON & CHINNOCKS

In conjunction with

ESCRITT & BARRELL

at the LONDON AUCTION MART, 155, Queen Victoria Street, E.C.4
on TUESDAY and WEDNESDAY, NOVEMBER 15th and 16th, 1949
at 2.30 p.m. precisely each day.

Solicitors :
Messrs. WITHERS & CO., Howard House, 4, Arundel Street, Strand, London, W.C.2
(Telephone : TEMple Bar 8400)

Auctioneers' Offices :
8, TELEGRAPH STREET, MOORGATE, LONDON, E.C.2
(Telephone : MONarch 5962)
ELMER HOUSE, GRANTHAM, LINCS
(Telephone : Grantham 1035)

Particulars of the Ham and Petersham estate auction sale, 15th and 16th November 1949

Opposite: The south front view of Ham House
Photo by David Yates

leased to Leyland) would be a bomb target. The safe deposits were blitzed and subsequently flooded by fire-fighting hoses. The papers were not removed for some time afterwards and by the time this was finally done considerable decomposition had set in.

Despite the 20th century development, the distinctive rural character of the two villages, with large expanses of river meadows and open spaces, has been largely maintained to this day.

Ham House, built in 1610 by Sir Thomas Vavasour, Knight Marshal to
James I, is one of the finest surviving Stuart houses in England. In spite of its
name, it is in fact in the parish of Petersham, though the grounds straddle the
Ham/Petersham boundary. Today it is a Grade I listed building in the care of
the National Trust.

In 1626 Ham House was the home of the Scotsman William Murray, one of
Charles I's inner circle of friends. He was ennobled in 1643, being created
1st Earl of Dysart and Viscount Huntingtower. His eldest daughter Elizabeth,
Countess of Dysart in her own right, married Sir Lionel Tollemache in 1648
and it is from this union that the subsequent Earls of Dysart of Ham House
are descended. Her second marriage to the Earl (later Duke) of Lauderdale
took place in 1672 at St Peter's Church. He was Secretary of State for Scotland
and a key member of the 'CABAL' ministry that formed Charles II's inner
cabinet. The word CABAL is an acronym of the initials of the five royalists
who were Charles II's chief ministers between 1668 and 1674. Ham House
thus became a centre of political intrigue and power during the Restoration.

Ham Polo Club

Ham House

Rifle & Pistol Club

The Palm Centre

Old Ham Lodge

The Orangery

Manor House

Beaufort House

Wiggins and Pointers Cottages

Royal Oak public house

Newman House

Grey Court School

Ham Library

Ham Close

Wates estate

Tollemache Almshouses

Stokes House and Bench House

Selby House

St Richard's Church

St Thomas Aquinas Church

Boxall Cottages

The Malt House and Ensleigh Lodge

Ham Common and Pond

The Little House

Gordon House

Ham Institute

Forbes House

Langham House and Langham House Close

The Gate House

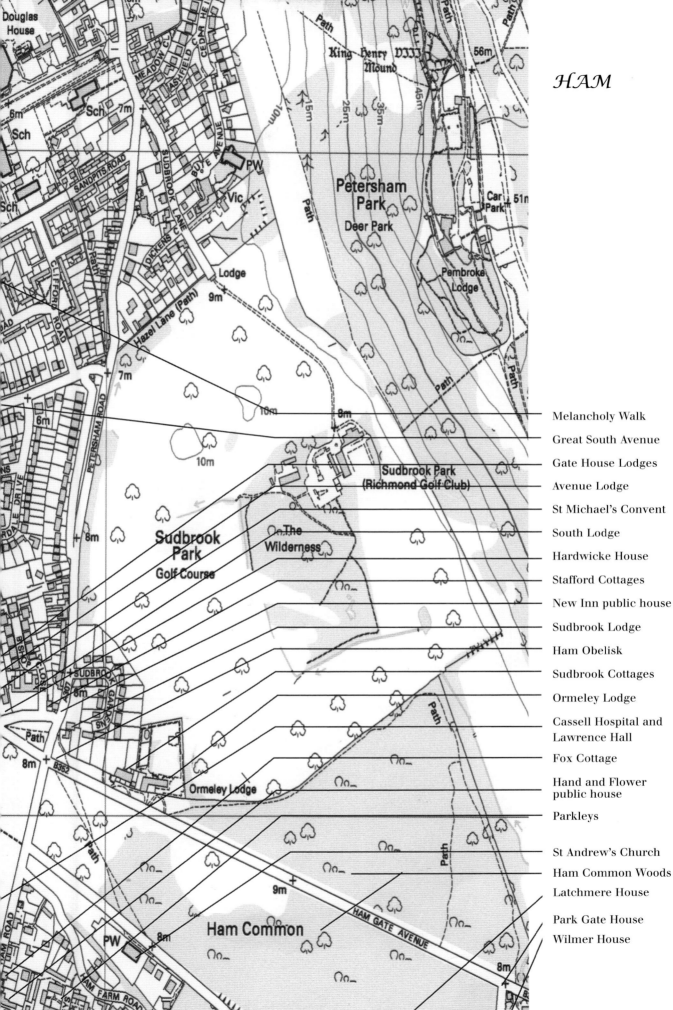

HAM

Melancholy Walk

Great South Avenue

Gate House Lodges

Avenue Lodge

St Michael's Convent

South Lodge

Hardwicke House

Stafford Cottages

New Inn public house

Sudbrook Lodge

Ham Obelisk

Sudbrook Cottages

Ormeley Lodge

Cassell Hospital and
Lawrence Hall

Fox Cottage

Hand and Flower
public house

Parkleys

St Andrew's Church

Ham Common Woods

Latchmere House

Park Gate House

Wilmer House

13

The Duke and Duchess of Lauderdale enlarged the house and embarked on a lavish refurbishment, the results of which can still be seen today along with many of the pictures and furniture they commissioned at that time. The house thus provides a rare opportunity to see interiors which have survived largely intact since the late 17th century.

The Avenues around Ham House were laid out by the Duchess at the same time as the enlargements were made to the house in about 1679: they offered ornamental and formal walks as an extension of the garden itself. Today they are an exceptional example of landscape survival from this period. They are shown clearly on John Rocque's map of about 1746 and the earlier 'Helmingham Plan' of 1740.

In 1678 John Evelyn wrote in his journal:
'After dinner I walked to Ham to see the House and garden of the Duke of Lauderdale, which is indeed inferior to few of the best villas in Italy itself; the House furnished like a great Prince; the Parterres, Flower Gardens, Orangeries, Groves, Avenues, Courts, Statues, Perspectives, Fountains, Aviaries and all this at the banks of the Sweetest River in the World, must needs be surprising.'

The main approach to Ham House in the 17th and much of the 18th century was from the Thames, by boat. Carriages and horses would have arrived from Ham Street to the stables on the west side of the house.

In 1834 Barbara Hofland wrote of Ham House:
'The beautiful groves and walks which environ the mansion have been celebrated by many of our poets. The fine and stately row of shadowy elms, which adorn the banks of the river, casts a refreshing coolness over the stilly surface of the stream, and, in softening and harmonizing the feelings, prepare them more fully to relish all the various beauties of sylvan scenery displayed on reaching the lovely village of Petersham and the commanding heights of Richmond Hill.'

Above: Ham House Stables built at the same time as Ham House c.1610 with later additions on the east side in 1787

Opposite: The Duke and Duchess of Lauderdale, by Sir Peter Lely (1618–80),
Ham House, the Dysart Collection
The National Trust
©NTPL/John Bethell

Opposite: A photo of the majestic elm trees of the Great South Avenue taken from the Upper Ham Road c.1929
*Reproduced by kind permission of
Sir David Williams*

This page: *Joan walking down one of the Ham Avenues,* from an oil painting by her husband Tony Rampton,1983

There was once an avenue that extended west, in front of Ham House, across the flood meadows almost to the river Thames, now called the *Great River Avenue*. The *Great South Avenue* runs from the south gate of Ham House to and across the open part of Ham Common. Adjacent to the house on the east side is *Melancholy Walk*. These two are linked by a third avenue called the *Petersham Avenue* which runs east alongside the Polo Club and the German School to the Arched Lodge on the Petersham Road. Melancholy Walk is shown on early plans as being planted in the quincunx, a fashionable mid-eighteenth century method of planting trees in a domino five pattern.

Ralph Thoresby (1658–1725), the topographer and antiquary from Leeds and a visitor in 1712, wrote:
'We walked through the delicate meadows near the river and trees artfully planted in the quincunx order making agreeable views and walks in different ways.'

It is thought that the Avenues were originally planted with some lime but mostly elm trees. Considered to be an ideal tree for formal avenues, in maturity elms reach a height of around 130 feet and have a lifespan of over 250 years. Often meeting overhead, they must have made a dramatic sight, and gave out a strong message – a reminder of the power and authority of the Lord of the Manor.

As a continuation of the twin rows of elms on the common were the lovely avenues to Ham House with the stately trees meeting overhead in places. The avenues were fenced on both sides with white palings, and at each end of the two avenues from Ham Common to Ham House were carriage gates and kissing gates. Similar gates were at the Ham Street entrance to the Ham House grounds and carriage gates still exist. The Petersham entrance to the avenues was guarded, and still is, by a fine Lodge, and I think was the main entrance; and here in these quiet avenues cows grazed and owls hooted and called from the trees. The property was kept in fine condition by Lord Dysart, as was a gravel path laid in the avenue between Ham Common and Sandy Lane. It was a privilege allowed to local people to use this path to reach the river – a privilege which was never abused.

'Reminiscences' by Marjorie Lansdale

At one time the Ham Avenues, or Ham Walks as they were known, were kept locked by the Dysarts and only a privileged few were allowed a key to gain access. In the early 1950s however, the ownership of the Avenues and Petersham Copse were conveyed to the Borough of Richmond by the Dysart estate. The Avenue trees were in a dilapidated state and considered to be

Above: A watercolour of one of the Ham Avenues c.1842 by Lady Caroline Lucy Scott who lived at Douglas House in Petersham. This is most probably Petersham Avenue facing east towards the Petersham Road before the Arched Lodge was built. (see page 104)
Reproduced by kind permission of James Gibson

Opposite: The Great South Avenue today, looking north towards Ham House.

The Avenue of Trees at Ham
by John Constable, RA
According to his letters, Constable was a frequent visitor to Louisa Manners, the 7th Countess of Dysart, between 1812 and 1834. He often walked in the gardens and grounds around Ham House and sketched this pencil drawing in 1834
©*V&A Images/Victoria and Albert Museum, London*

The South Gates to Ham House, 1941 by John Sanderson-Wells for the Recording Britain Collection
©*V&A Images/Victoria and Albert Museum, London*

dangerous. In 1953 it was agreed that most of the trees along the Petersham Avenue and the northern part of the Great South Avenue should be felled and replanted with lime trees by local schoolchildren. Dutch elm disease took its toll in the 1960s and 70s and for many years thereafter the Avenues received little maintenance.

Fortunately, in 2001 English Heritage awarded this historical landscape a Grade II* listing in their Register of Parks and Gardens, and following an initiative started by the Thames Landscape Strategy in 1991, Kim Wilkie, a well-known landscape architect, produced a restoration plan that balanced nature conservation, historic landscape and public access concerns. The proposals were mostly put into effect by the London's Arcadia project and in 2007–9 the Avenues have been restored after years of neglect.

The ornamental gates which lead from the south gardens of Ham House to the Great South Avenue carry the coat of arms of the Earls of Dysart surrounded by the words *Nemo me impune lacessit* (No one provokes me with impunity). This is the motto of the Most Ancient and Noble Order of the Thistle, which was created in 1687 and conferred on the 4th Earl of Dysart (1708–70).

On the nearby Petersham Copse there are many magnificent old oaks probably dating from the early 18th century. They are depicted on the John Rocque map on page 6. We can only speculate as to why these grand old oaks were spared the woodman's axe and survive to this day; they are now sadly swamped by impenetrable undergrowth and largely unnoticed.

Ham Lands, or Ham Fields as they were also known, cover a 200-acre area from Ham Street in the east to the bend of the river in the west. Much of the land was traditionally grazed flood meadows; there are remains of a tiny Anglo-Saxon hamlet which was called Coldharbour in the northern part of the Lands. The land, owned by the Lords of the Manor, was farmed on the Open Field system of agriculture. In the late 19th century much of the land was made over to the growing of fruit and vegetables. The 1902 Richmond, Petersham and Ham Open Spaces Act extinguished the Lammas Rights (see page 33) of the inhabitants of Ham and freed much of Ham Lands for the profitable business of large-scale gravel extraction. At the same time the new Teddington Lock, the upstream limit of the tidal Thames, was constructed in place of earlier locks and this reduced the frequency of flooding on the Lands.

The Ham River Grit Company was duly granted a lease to extract gravel from the Ham Lands, and operations started in 1904. A wharf and processing plant were constructed and barges carried the gravel away. The Thames Young Mariners today use the lagoon from which the barges were loaded. The gravel extraction continued until just before the Second World War, by which time a large area of the Lands had been worked. It was backfilled with bomb-damage spoil and rubble, and with ballast from development areas such as London's South Bank. When the infilling finished, the land could not be developed by law for a number of years in order to reduce the risk of subsidence. The future of the 60-acre gravel pits site was the subject of two well-attended public meetings in 1959 and 1960, held by the Ham and Petersham Association, and eventually planning permission was granted and soon new houses were built on the Ham Wates estate on the eastern side of Riverside Drive.

A further 33 acres of Ham Lands on the western side, towards the river, were owned by the Ham River Grit Company. It was also proposed to develop this land with social housing. It was not until 1983 that the Ham Lands Action Committee, under the auspices of the

Ham and Petersham Association and led by the Ward Councillor David Williams, now Sir David, managed to secure most of this area as Metropolitan Open Land and safe from building. Only the Locksmeade estate on the south-west side was developed in 1983. Today (2009), the remaining open area of Ham Lands alongside the river is designated as a local nature reserve. The risk of flooding here, and in some lower lying areas of Petersham, is expected to increase in future as the climate changes, because of the combined effect of rising sea levels and more tidal surges with freshwater flooding and the inflow of water from increased urban drainage. To counter this threat there are plans to restore the naturally functioning floodplain and to re-establish wetland habitats for wildlife.

The Anglican Church of St Richard in the centre of the Wates estate was consecrated by the Bishop of Kingston in 1966. The Bishop was unable to find a Surrey saint to name the church so he chose St Richard de Wyche, Bishop of Chichester in Sussex in the 13th century. It was built to an unusual plan based on the Star of David and roofed with an interesting geometrical structure. The architects were Covell, Matthews and Partners.

A ferry has linked Ham to Twickenham since the late 17th century. The ferrymen paid annual rental to the Lords of the Manor, the Dysarts, who also collected tolls from users of the towpath from Teddington to Richmond. Threepence was charged for each horse until the towpath was put under the control of the Richmond Corporation in 1902. In 1908 a licensed waterman, Walter Hammerton from Twickenham, started a new passenger ferry service across the river; he also provided boats and punts for hire. Hammerton took objection to having to pay a license fee to the Dysarts for the new ferry. After a bitter battle and protracted court cases, Hammerton eventually successfully appealed to the House of Lords. A ferry still operates here today.

The Ham and Petersham Rifle and Pistol Club is a private shooting club situated between Riverside Drive and the Ham playing fields; it was established in the early 1900s as a rifle range. During the First World War it was used for army training and over 24,000 recruits took firing courses there.

Old Ham Lodge on the Ham Green triangle is a historic building closely associated with the Dysart estate. It most probably began life as a 'bothy' (almost unfurnished accommodation) for farm labourers or

Hay making at Secrett's Farm west of Ham Street

The interior of the old Manor Farm barn

These watercolours were painted in 1941 by John
Sanderson-Wells for the Recording Britain Collection
©*V&A Images/Victoria and Albert Museum, London*

apprentice gardeners at Ham House. It may date from as early as the 18th century. It was sold in 1949 in the estate auction. The old kitchen gardens of Ham House adjoining the Lodge now have a new lease of life as the Palm Centre nursery. The small alleyway that leads from Ham Street past the Palm Centre to the Great South Avenue just south of the gates to Ham House is worryingly named Cut Throat Alley.

In 1861 Ham Manor Farm or Hatch's Farm covered an area of 306 acres, stretching down from the west side of Ham Street, behind Beaufort House, all the way to the river. At that time the tenant farmer was William Hatch; the Secrett family took over the farm tenancy in 1918. The Channel Island dairy cows they kept on the riverside meadows were herded south down Ham Street for their daily milking at the farm. Gradually the farm land was sold off and by 1929 the farm was reduced to 70 acres. After the Second World War, 100 prefabs were erected on what is now Ham Close to cater for housing needs, particularly of returning servicemen. Originally blocks of flats were planned, including one block of nine storeys, but fortunately, due to the opposition of the Ham and Petersham Association and others who objected to such large-scale development which would destroy the character of the small village, the project was delayed and a compromise was reached, the development eventually being reduced to five, four and three-storey blocks. In 1957 Lou Secrett relinquished the farm and the rest of the land was given up to make way for this Ham Close development. The Manor farmhouse was demolished in 1958, and in the process a much earlier farmhouse and barn were discovered and very sadly destroyed: under the brick and stucco there had been a 15th century three-bay hall with Gothic windows, leaded lights and 1ft square oak beams.

The farmhouse was replaced by the Borough Council with 13 units of shops, with flats above (opposite Grey Court School). This could well be described as Ham's most undesirable development, an example of urban design at its worst. Today several of the shops are often boarded up or empty, making the whole episode, starting with the destruction of the ancient farmhouse, an object lesson in the results of poor planning.

The original Ham Manor House was built some time during Queen Anne's reign (1702–14), but was greatly enlarged on the garden side by J Compton-Hall in 1908. This magnificent house stands in extensive grounds bordering on the Great South Avenue to Ham House; there is a *ha-ha* in the garden which used to divide the lawn from the field and also marks the Petersham and Ham boundary. In the late 1970s the walled vegetable garden, to the north of the house on Ham Street, was sold off to build a sixteen-house development known as The Orangery. Originally, the proposal had been to sell off a much larger area of land for development, including part of the former meadow land adjacent to the Great South Avenue south of Ham House. A Ham and Petersham Association Committee member, James Batten, gave extensive evidence about the historical and environmental importance of the site at a planning inquiry in 1973. With the support of many amenity and conservation societies, he succeeded in convincing the inquiry inspector of the merits of his case, and the housing development was restricted to a smaller area which did not impinge on the Avenue or on the setting of Ham House.

In 1712 Ham Manor House was owned by William Genew who by 1727 also had a large estate to the north of Ham Common, where Avenue Lodge and St Michael's Convent now stand.

Above: The Manor House, Ham Street and the geese in the garden

Right: Sir George Gilbert Scott
oil painting by George Richmond c.1870
©*RIBA Library Drawing Collection*

Far Right: Oil painting of Sir Everard Home
by Thomas Phillips 1820
©*The Royal Society*

Left: The Palm Centre Nursery once part of the kitchen gardens of Ham House

During the 19th century there was a succession of well-known occupants; in 1819 the eminent surgeon Sir Everard Home (1756–1832) and his wife Dame Jane (who was buried at St Peter's in 1841) lived here. Brother-in-law and pupil of the famous surgeon John Hunter, he assisted Hunter in many of his anatomical investigations, although it was claimed that he plagiarised Hunter's work. Home was elected to the Royal Society of Surgeons in 1785 and was sergeant-surgeon to Kings George III, George IV, and William IV. He was created a baronet in 1813 and appointed surgeon to Chelsea Hospital in 1821. This became his official residence, and he died there in 1832.

Sir Everard wrote the following to his midshipman son, of the same name, on Friday, 4 January 1822:

'. . . . *I have this moment my dear Everard received your letter which I answer immediately to save the Post. You have had bad luck but not so bad as all the neighbourhood of Ham. Many are living upstairs supplied by Boats with provisions; so completely is the country flooded. Our house and grounds have completely escaped . . . .*'

And on the following Thursday night:

'. . . . *I have the satisfaction to tell you that our Ham neighbours have once more got upon dry land, and what is still more satisfactory, that no part of our premises have been in the least affected by these floods. Petersham lane,*

Opposite: The Manor House from the front

Above: Gate architectural detail at the Manor House

Below: Cows walking down Ham Street outside the Manor House painted in 1941 by John Sanderson-Wells for the Recording Britain Collection
©*V&A Images/Victoria and Albert Museum, London*

between Sandy lane and the Common, was under water several days; but Sandy-lane itself continued, through its whole length, high and dry; and there is no trial by water which the premises are likely to undergo that can put them in the least danger. This is what could not have been expected.'

He was describing the 'Great Flood' that started in December 1821, when the highest flood levels ever were recorded at Teddington. The worst flood on the non-tidal Thames in recent history occurred in November 1894 and was due to exceptionally heavy rainfall; it was followed by another in March 1947, which also caused much flooding in the city of London itself.

In years gone by, it was not uncommon for the river Thames to freeze over, as it did notably in January 1814, after a long spell of cold and dry weather. Then the Thames was wider and shallower so that the water flowed more slowly, but today the river flow is said to be too fast to allow a total freeze.

In 1833 the Manor House was the home of Lord Dudley Coutts Stuart MP and his wife Princess Christine Bonaparte (see Bute House, page 96). It was also the

home, from 1864, of the architect Sir George Gilbert Scott, who spent the last 14 years of his life here, using the gardener's cottage in the grounds as his drawing office. A leading figure in the Gothic revival, Sir George was responsible for the Albert Memorial and St Pancras Station and Hotel. He also designed and built St Matthias' Church with its 200ft spire, a notable landmark in Richmond, and many other churches and public buildings. He died in 1878 and is buried in Westminster Abbey.

From 1895, the Manor House was the home of the three Hornby spinster sisters. Emily Hornby, the eldest, was an intrepid traveller and in 1907 published *Mountaineering Records*, a book about her travels, which began in 1873. The sisters were descendants of Thomas Dyson Hornby, a merchant from Northumberland, after whom the Liverpool dock opened in 1884 was named.

Major-General and Mrs Hermione McGrath lived here for many years. He was at one time a director of Wembley Stadium. She was a keen gardener and her gardens were open to the public under the National Gardens Scheme in the early 1960s.

Beaufort House, a fine and elegant brick house with a coach house and stables and a large garden to the south of the house, was built in about 1780. As with the Manor House opposite, it was once part of the Dysart estate. In 1795/6 for a short time it was the home of the author Sir Herbert Croft, who married into the Lewis family which had strong connections with Ham House, one of his wife's sisters, Magdalena, being married to the 5th Earl of Dysart and another sister, Anna Maria, being married to the 6th Earl.

In about 1837 it was the home of Harry Borradaile, whose son Edward, a graduate of Sandhurst, applied at the age of 28 for a position with the Northern Territory Administration of Australia. He was a civil engineer with experience of railway construction in Victoria and Tasmania. Borradaile and his older companion, Permain, an Irish-born surveyor, both of whom had mountains named after them, were reported missing while on an overland exploration looking for alluvial gold. It is thought that they were killed by aborigines. A brass memorial plaque in St Andrew's church has an engraving of the Northern Territory with the approximate position of where the explorers were last seen.

In 1847 the Revd Joseph France lived here and ran an independent school with five boy pupils. There is a tablet erected to his memory at St Andrew's church. The house later passed into use as a private Catholic school for girls, the School of St Elizabeth, which had transferred here from Carrington Lodge in Richmond. A mission chapel, known as St Mary's, was set up in the old stable block. In 1861 the school had a teaching staff of seven governesses and twenty-five resident pupils, many of them children of administrators or military personnel serving abroad in the British Empire. The school closed in 1870.

Eustace Neville Craig, who was chairman of the Ham Urban District Council for 16 years and its chairman from 1920 to 1926, lived here as did Count and Countess Lewenhaupt; his father was the Swedish and Norwegian Ambassador in London from 1895 to 1902.

In 1958 it was the home of Dr William Keith Badgett and his wife who both had a practice in St Margaret's and Isleworth. It was the Badgetts who sold, in the late 1950s, the kitchen garden to the south of the property later used for the housing development on Wiggins Lane. At the same time the northern kitchen wing of Beaufort House was converted to separate accommodation, called Beaufort Cottage. Yarrell's Cottage on the corner of Ham Street and Wiggins Lane was demolished in 1969 as the Ministry of Housing considered it unfit for human habitation; Linden House was built in its place.

There are two lead Firemarks above the front door of Beaufort House. The mark of the Hand-in-Hand Fire and Life Insurance Society, established in 1696, has the number of the policy stamped on the panel below the design. There is a similar one on the Manor House front wall on the opposite side of the road, and many others still exist on the older and larger houses in both Ham and Petersham. The second mark is of the Westminster Insurance Office established in 1717, though the usual Prince of Wales feathers above the portcullis are missing.

Opposite: A quiet corner of the garden at Beaufort House

The old school bell still exists on the northern wall

Lead Firemarks above the door

Beaufort House and porch detail

Newman House on Ham Street was previously called Grove House and Grey Court House and is the only building in Ham and Petersham to have a Blue Plaque. It was built in 1742 and was once the boyhood country home of Cardinal John Henry Newman (1801–90), the well-known English churchman. Now the house is part of the secondary school Grey Court which was opened in 1956. The Newman family lived in Southampton Street (now Southampton Place) in Bloomsbury and took over the house in Ham Street as a country retreat in about 1800. The eldest of six children, Newman was brought up in the Anglican faith. In his early life, he was a major figure in the Oxford Movement to bring the Church of England back to its Catholic roots, and the author of a number of influential books. He converted to Catholicism in 1845 and was posthumously proclaimed 'Venerable' by the Roman Catholic Church in 1991. At the time of writing (2009) the beatification of the Church of England's most significant convert to Roman Catholicism is under consideration. This would pave the way for Cardinal Newman to be made a saint – the first non-martyr saint in England since the Reformation.

When he was older Newman wrote about his boyhood home to a friend:
'I have been looking at the windows of our house at Ham near Richmond, where I lay aged five looking at the candles stuck in them in celebration of the victory of Trafalgar (October 21st, 1805). I have never seen the house since September 1807 – I know more about it than any house I have been in since, and could pass an examination on it. It has ever been in my dreams.'

The Royal Oak is a historic public house that was originally an abattoir for Manor Farm; it became an inn in the 1700s and retains much of its original architectural character and detail.

Opposite: Newman House

John Henry Newman in 1887

The Royal Oak public house
by John Sanderson-Wells, 1941
for the Recording Britain Collection
©V&A Images/Victoria and Albert Museum,
London

The Royal Oak public house today

This letter written by Queen Charlotte (1744-1818), wife of George III, about a visit to Ham, most probably to Grove House, may have been written to her daughter Princess Amelia on 7 September 1809. It is taken from a footnote in *The Letters and Correspondence of Mary Berry* (Vol. II, p.423).

'I am to thank My dearest . . . . for a very Kind Letter I received yesterday, and wished to have answered it immediately, but was prevented doing it by a Visit to Lady Caroline and Mrs. Damer at Ham, where we were received most kindly in Every Sense. This little retreat is quite a little Earthly Paradise; the House stands in a Green Field Incircled by Most Magnificent Trees all Planted by the late General Carpenter, a Gravel Walk goes all round the Shrubbery, and also round another Field which goes to the end of Ham walks, there they keep three Cows the produce of their Milck is sufficient for their Establishment. The House consists below Stairs of a small Hall, Drawing room and Dining room and a Small Parlour which is Lady Portarlington's Painting Room when she inhabits the House. The drawing and dining Room are entirely furnished with Lady Portarlington's Paintings consisting chiefly of Copies after the Old and most Famous Masters. A Picture of Her Mother in a Turkish Dress, one of the Present Lord Bute, and one of Sir Charles Stewart are those not done by Her. From the Salle de Companie you go into the Gardens where under the shade of the finest Trees possible you may save Yourself from the Violence of the Sun. Above Stairs there are upon the Best Floor four excellent Bed Chambers, and Mrs. Damer assures me that the Attics are good and the offices also. We dined at three and had the honour of Mrs. Damer's Housekeeper and Cook as Elegant and good a Dinner as if a Cordon Bleue had directed it, we were very Cheerful and a little after four we drank Coffé; the rain having ceased Lady Caroline wished to shew me from Ham walks the View of the River and likewise that of Lord Dysart's Place and as she has been favoured with a key she offered to carry us there, we walked and most delightful it was there, and saw not only the House, but all the beautiful Old China which a Civil Housekeeper offered to shew us.' (A description of the contents of Ham House follows.) 'We returned by six to Ham, and left Our Hostesses and Lady Cardigan immediately, we were back time enough to dress before the King returned from London.'

Ham Library was built in 1952 on the site of the old Manor Farm Orchard. Next door, tucked behind their fences, are two flat-roofed bungalows, numbers 57 and 59 Ham Street, designed by the Hungarian-born architect Stefan Buzás, who founded James Cubitt & Partners. They were built in 1951 and although now much altered are widely considered to be good examples of the purest form of modern domestic architecture. Buzás also built the New House on Church Road.

The redbrick and terracotta Tollemache Almshouses in Ham Street were endowed and erected by the wife of Algernon Tollemache MP as a memorial to him when he died in 1891. He was the brother of the 8th Earl of Dysart and one of the three trustees of the Dysart estate. The six almshouses provide accommodation for nine people, three of them being designed for married couples and three for single people.

Stokes Hall, now divided into Stokes House and the Bench House, was built in the Georgian period, with some later additions. In the 1850s it was a boarding school for girls between 6 and 19 years of age, run by the Barker sisters, Sarah, Ann and Charlotte. It was then purchased by the Dysarts in about 1875 and let to a succession of occupants. Dr Arthur Charles Baggley, the local GP, lived there for 21 years from 1931. It was finally sold in the 1949 Ham and Petersham estate auction and in 1972 separated into the two houses we see today. The Bench, a group of houses to the north-west of Stokes Hall, was a small freehold property of ten tenements, reduced to five prior to 1896. They were purchased by the Dysarts and included in the 1949 auction with Stokes Hall. They were demolished in 1964 when they were said to have been over 200 years old. With outside privies and having no hot water, they were considered unfit for human habitation. New houses have been built on the site.

Ham Street will have started life as a path or trackway leading from the Richmond – Kingston road to the river, used by fishermen, boatmen and farm workers taking a reasonably direct route over the flat land, with diversions to follow field and property boundaries where these existed. This track formed a natural focus for building development as the local population grew over the years. Ham Street was originally straight, but Katherine, the wife of William Murray, 1st of Earl Dysart diverted it (probably to build a large barn) to its present course. Her daughter Elizabeth, Countess of Dysart, and Sir Lionel Tollemache caused a deed to be enrolled in the Richmond manor court records in 1652 guaranteeing 'for all time' that the new route should be 'a common way for all uses'. Back Lane, parallel to Ham Street on the west side, was a later development, linking the village to its farms and fields.

Above: The Tollemache Almshouses, erected in memory of Algernon Tollemache in 1891

Below: Wiggins Cottages are named after William Wiggins, a gardener and grocer who had a shop in Back Lane. He died in 1867

Some of the earliest surviving cottages are those on the eastern side of Ham Street near the Common, which were built about 1820, the next developments being Wiggins Cottages which were built in the mid 1800s on the corner of Back Lane and Ham Street just north of the junction with Sandy Lane. William Wiggins was a gardener and grocer and owned a shop in Back Lane. Soon afterwards Pointers Cottages were built next to Wiggins Cottages, named after John Pointer, a coachbuilder from Central London.

Above: Winson's Supply Stores in about 1915. It became Fieldson's Stores or the Supply Stores in the 1930s and then after the Second World War the London Co-operative Society Stores, which were run by Mr Cox. It is now known as the Old Bakery at number 11 Ham Street

Celebration of the Coronation in 1911. This photo shows the procession of young children alongside the Ham National School, now St Thomas Aquinas Church
Reproduced by kind permission of the Local Studies Library, Richmond

Right: The Malt House in the early 1900s, now all that remains of the house and farm of 115 acres
Below, the house today

Below: A copy of the entry in the Ham National Girls' School log-book which records, in elegant script, a summary of H. M. Inspector's Report for 1892

Opposite: Ham Street from the Common by John Sanderson-Wells, 1941 for the Recording Britain Collection
©*V&A Images/Victoria and Albert Museum, London*

The school houses on Ham Street and St Thomas Aquinas Church

Sep. 20th 1892
Copy of the Summary of H. M. Inspector's Report.

Girls' School. "The school has passed a fairly satisfactory examination. Reading is good. Dictation is on the whole very fair. Arithmetic is extremely weak, especially in the upper standards.
Domestic Economy is only fairly well answered. Needlework is some of it good, the rest rather ordinary. The samples worked for examination are considered fair. Songs are pleasingly sung, the note tests fully satisfied. The children's behaviour, appearance, and attention to their studies are quite exemplary."

In the late 19th century more cottages were added as Ham developed quickly from a small hamlet to a proper village with the arrival of many tradesmen and smallholders. A complete new street of 18 small terraced houses, Evelyn Road, was added in about 1884, with four more houses, Evelyn Terrace, nearby in Ham Street itself, now even numbers 40–46.

Some of the cottages accommodated small tradesmen from time to time, including a shoemaker, a confectioner near Ham Common, and another on the corner of Evelyn Road. Other shops were purpose-built and in the 1895 Kelly Directory there is a listing for Holmwood's Stores at number 10 Ham Street, a grocery store owned by Ernest Ichabod Holmwood who also owned the cottage next door, number 8. Both these buildings have now gone but the cottage where Harry Dunkley and his wife first started trading as confectioners and tobacconists, number 12, still remains. The Trades Directories from 1890 to the 1920s show that there were also a butcher, baker, boot and shoe makers, draper, wheelwright, carpenters, greengrocers and a smithy. The Dunkleys continued trading as Ham General Stores at number 12 until after the Second World War, then moving the shop to its present site at numbers 31–33. This was the site of the original village inn The Crooked Billet which in 1935 had moved to a new position south along the street towards the Common, opposite the Ham Brewery Tap public house, at numbers 13–23. It was finally demolished in 1996 to make way for new terraced houses.

In 1936 the Dysart family estates were transferred to Buckminster Estates Ltd, a family company, which was listed as occupying number 2 Ham Street in 1948. The company was wound up in 1949, in the same year as the estate auction.

Home Farm, at the Ham Street end of what is now Lock Road, was another major farm in Ham in the 19th century. The Light family were the farmers and maltsters, growing flax in abundance in the adjacent fields. As with the other two farms in Ham (Manor Farm and Ham Farm Nursery) the land was owned by the Dysarts and leased to the farmers.

The site of St Thomas Aquinas Church was originally that of two almshouses. In 1817 a school room was built above them. In 1846 the almshouses were moved and the old buildings converted to school use. They were pulled down when the school was rebuilt in 1876–7 to become Ham's first local school, known as St Andrew's National School. It was run by the parish with places for 101 boys and 74 girls as well as a number of infants. The log books for the school have been saved and are now stored at the Local Studies Library in Richmond town centre. The houses on the opposite side of Ham Street were school houses provided for the teachers. In July 1966 permission was given by the London Borough of Richmond for the use of the building as a Church (Chapel of Ease) and Hall, and from that date it was administered as St Thomas Aquinas Roman Catholic Church and Parish Hall.

1900s photo of Lock Road looking towards Ham Common. As with many of the roads in Ham, Lock Road followed the line of an old path that once went down as far as Teddington Lock. The part of the road that runs from Craig Road to Ham Common was constructed in about 1890. By 1934 it extended all the way to Broughton Avenue. *Reproduced by kind permission of Sir David Williams*

Below: Selby House

Opposite: A poster for the Ham Races, dated Tuesday, August 21, 1821

Selby House was probably built in about 1688 and may have once been a farmhouse. It stands on an area known as Brymswych Close, two acres of land which stretched north from the house towards Sandy Lane. The house was purchased by the Duke of Argyll at the beginning of the 18th century. He added the third storey and encased the whole structure with red rubbed bricks. Selby House was acquired from him by Nicholas Hardinge, Lord of the Manor of Kingston Canbury, and he and his son George lived here until 1772. As with the nearby Gordon, Orford, and Beaufort Houses and Stokes Hall, Selby House became a boarding school in the mid 19th century. It was run by Edward Rolfe and his wife and there were 20 pupils aged from 5 to 16 years. Over the period 1889–1953 Selby House was the home of four generations of the Noble family. Alfred Noble and his son's family moved to Selby in 1889. Joseph Horace Noble was a solicitor and a well-known figure in the community until his death in 1913. He was on the Committee of Management for the Ham National School, next door to his house. His son Archie was killed in the First World War at Vimy Ridge and his daughter Mary married Kenneth Field, one of the 14 children of Joshua Field who lived at Latchmere House. Kenneth was also killed in Cambrai, France in 1917 and Mary and her two daughters went to live with her mother at Selby House. Mary stayed there until 1953, when she went to live with one of her daughters in Woking. She died at the age of 100 in 1988.

In 1891 the Dysart Trustees faced much local protest when they unsuccessfully attempted to claim Ham Common as their own Manor land. For many years the inhabitants of Ham had freely exercised their commoners' rights to graze animals, gather firewood, and collect game. Lawyers had had some difficulty in interpreting Charles I's 1635 Deed of Gift over the question of whether or not the 'waste' or common land was actually independent of all manorial claims. In 1891 protest erupted when the Trustees erected notice boards on Ham Common forbidding the removal of wood, game or gravel, and claimed that the common fields and footpaths were private property. A 'Ham Common Prosecutions Defence Committee' was formed, notice boards were chopped down, and four local men were prosecuted for felony. The men were triumphantly acquitted by a jury. The campaign was led by the 'champion of Ham' William Harry Harland, whose account *Ham Common and the Dysarts: a Brief and an Indictment* published in 1894 gives a detailed story of the struggle.

In parallel with this conflict, the Dysart Trustees were also seeking to deprive the local inhabitants of their Lammas Rights over the Ham Fields so as to free the land for development. These rights were a relic of the old Open Field system of agriculture, whereby land was enclosed and held in severalty (sole ownership) during the crop-growing season but thrown open to the commoners for pasturage or grazing from Lammas Day – originally celebrating the start of the harvest festival on 1st August – for the rest of the year. Lammas Rights had been little used for some time as from the late 19th century almost all the fields had been made over for market-garden cultivation, but the commoners understandably resented the Trustees' high-handed and self-seeking schemes. The position was finally resolved by the 1902 Richmond, Petersham and Ham Open Spaces Act whereby the view from Richmond Hill was preserved, many open spaces in Ham and Petersham together with the riverside towpath were vested in Richmond Corporation for public enjoyment, and the commoners' Lammas Rights over the Ham Lands were finally extinguished.

Ham Common is once a year a gay scene, as a fair is held there merely for the purposes of sport, and much frequented not only by the neighbouring rustics but those of higher rank, whose carriages are frequently seen waiting in the vicinity whilst the owners amuse themselves with the humours of the place. It is too great a distance from the metropolis to become liable to those disorders which have rendered meetings of this kind such general subjects of complaint, and we therefore hope it will not be included in those plans of reform which are wisely adopted under other circumstances. The loud laughter of the sportive childhood, the warm meetings of humble but hearty friends, the relaxation from toil, which imparts a pleasure the labourer alone can know, and compresses into a few smiling hours all the luxuries poverty can hope to enjoy, are circumstances so pleasant to witness or contemplate, that few persons would desire to check the harmless hilarity of a such a spectacle, more especially when it is beheld under the beams of a summer sky, and surrounded by the beauties of a country so fair as this.

Writing this in 1832, Barbara Hofland was describing the Fair that took place on the Common on the Whit Bank Holiday weekend in May each year; the Ham horse and pony races were also held here each August. There were, however, rumblings of discontent. The legality of the races was called into question and, according to parish records, extra watchmen and village constables had to be employed to patrol the parish to prevent theft and damage to property. The races ceased in 1868, apparently because they attracted too many undesirable characters.

William Brockwell (1866–1935), known as 'Brockie', was the club's most outstanding cricketer. In the 1880s he notably took ten wickets for three runs. He played for Surrey County Cricket Club and for England. At the end of his career, until 1911, he lived at Rajinder Cottage on Ham Common. His father was a blacksmith and the family owned cottages in Ham Street as well as the Boxall Cottages on Ham Common

This charming watercolour of Ham Pond by William Luker was painted in about 1892. It shows the original oak framed Malt House topped with its louvred ventilator, demolished in 1906 to make way for Lock Road to run straight on to the Common. Ensleigh Lodge with its interesting façade is described by Pevsner as 'a cottage of c.1800, with lower wings with a double-curved top to reach the walls of the cottage, and two solid wood fanlights'. The Little House is behind the tree on the left

Cricket has been played regularly on the Common since the early 19th century. The original cricket club in Ham was called the Albion Club, then the Ham Albion and in 1868 it was re-named Ham Star and finally the Ham and Petersham Cricket Club in 1891. The club held its meetings variously at the Crooked Billet in Ham Street, the Ham Institute in New Road and the Hand and Flower public house which stands next door to the cricket pavilion on the Upper Ham Road. Annual dinners were held at the New Inn; the cost of the cricket club dinner in 1906 was three shillings a head.

In the 1920s after a cricket match, 'Married versus the Singles', a tug of war took place across the Pond. Each contestant was repeatedly dragged through mud and water, much to the amusement of the spectators. More recently a Summer Horticultural show was held each year on the Common, and today a well-attended summer Fair is still held there annually, organised by the Ham Amenities Group.

Today the open part of Ham Common is the centrepiece of Ham village. It has an informal village-green character and is surrounded by a remarkable collection of Georgian and later mansions of high-quality architecture, together with attractive groups of smaller houses and cottages. The village pond sits on the north-west corner of the Common. It has played a part in village life as a watering place for livestock for hundreds of years; the villagers also exercised their ancient rights as commoners to keep a cow, horse or sheep on the Common, an activity that continued until the 1930s. Often animals got stuck in the pond and had to be helped out. In 1987 devastation was caused by the great storm and many trees around the Common were lost.

Opposite: Ham Pond today

Cows grazing on the Common c.1920
Reproduced by kind permission of Sir David Williams

Two early 1900 photos of Ham Pond

A frosty morning on the Common, 1981
Photo by David Yates

THE POND, HAM COMMON.

But it was not until the late 1990s that steps were taken to make improvements to the pond as a natural wildlife habitat. For many years it had been neglected and used as a general dump. Local residents, led by the Ham and Petersham Association, successfully applied for grant funding from the Local Heritage Initiative Fund, which together with generous local contributions enabled them to reinstate the island, stabilise the banks and fully restore and plant around the pond in 2002. Now a haven for wildfowl and wildlife it has also become the regular home of mute swans that have enthralled visitors by nesting here and raising their cygnets. Residents continue to maintain and look after the pond on a regular basis.

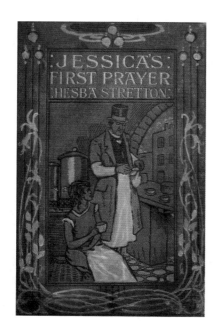

The front cover of an early edition of
Jessica's First Prayer by Hesba Stretton

The Little House on the corner of New Road and Ham Common was once called Laurel Cottage (when it was much smaller, in the 1840s) and also Ivycroft. Hesba Stretton and her sister Elizabeth moved here in 1890; Hesba died in 1911 and is buried at St Andrew's. Hesba's real name was Sarah Smith; in 1858 she adopted the pseudonym made up from the initial letters of the names of her brothers and sisters. Born in 1832, Hesba was a popular children's author of the day; her best known book was *Jessica's First Prayer* which sold one and a half million copies and was translated into many languages. Her stories are very moral and religious. She was appalled at the plight of the country's thousands of impoverished children at the time and with Baroness Burdett-Coutts helped to found what was later known as the NSPCC.

Her first literary success was due in part to her sister Elizabeth who sent Sarah's story *The Lucky Leg* to Charles Dickens who was then editing *Household Words.* Dickens liked the story, paid Sarah five pounds, and asked for more. She became a regular contributor to the magazine as a result and a friend of Dickens.

The building of New Road in the late 1870s made a big contribution to the steady expansion of Ham in the Victorian era. The Ham Institute, formerly the Working Men's Club, was originally an unlicensed club that was built for the working people of the village. In 1932 the Institute became for a time the Ham Parish Church Hall.

From the 1770s the houses and land on the south-west side of the Common, with the exception of the present Cassel Hospital site, were collectively known as the Ham Common estate; it was eventually sold to the Dysarts in 1893.

Gordon House, with its commanding position overlooking Ham Pond, was probably built in the latter half of the 17th century, with subsequent Georgian additions. The John Rocque map (see page 6) shows a house on the site, but this is probably a small farmhouse. It may have been named after General Gordon Forbes (1738–1828), of Skellator, Aberdeenshire, who lived at the house for about 50 years. He had a distinguished military career, serving in the American War and in the East and West Indies. The General and his wife Margaret had a large family of five sons and five daughters. Both the General and his wife died here, he at the age of 90, and were buried at St Peter's.

For a time in the mid 1800s William May ran a boys' school here, and in 1893 the house was bought by the Dysarts along with the rest of the Ham Common estate and subsequently leased.

In 1929 it was leased to Alan Bott, MC (1893–1952). In 1916 he had joined the 70th *('Umpty')* squadron of the Royal Flying Corps. His aircraft was shot down and he was captured by the Turks in 1918 but succeeded in making his escape, an event he wrote about in his book *Eastern Flights*. He later became the editor of The Graphic (1926–1932), and established the Reprint Society in 1939. In 1944 he founded Pan Books, the paperback publishers, with the aim of producing *'the best possible books at the lowest possible cost'*. He also assisted Charles Ede in setting up the Folio Society.

The house was sold by the Dysarts in the 1949 Ham and Petersham estate auction. For eleven years from 1954 it was the home of Doreen, Dowager Marchioness of Linlithgow, the widow of the 2nd Marquis, Viceroy of India from 1936 to 1943; it was she who created the fine garden which was eventually partly sold off for the development of Mornington Walk in 1967, when the house was sold by auction on her death.

In 1967 Gordon House was bought by Ralph Vernon-Hunt, a director of Pan Books and a relation of Alan Bott. He was depicted on some of the paperback book covers, designed by Sam Peffer, of the James Bond titles written by Ian Fleming that Pan produced so successfully between 1957 and 1962.

There have been at least three houses on the site of Forbes House. The original Georgian house was of a rather severe and bleak appearance. It was occupied by the 2nd Earl of Edgcumbe in the early 19th century. He married Lady Sophia, one of the daughters of John Hobart, 2nd Earl of Buckinghamshire.

Their daughter Emma Sophia, who later became Countess Brownlow, records visiting her father's villa on Ham Common in 1802/3 in her *Slight Reminiscences of a Septuagenarian* published in 1867. During the Napoleonic Wars in May 1803 Britain revoked the Treaty of Amiens and declared war on France. Bonaparte resumed plans for a military invasion of England, a threat which continued for two more years until Nelson's victory at Trafalgar in October 1805. She writes that this *'aroused all the national patriotism and volunteer corps were everywhere formed. Even Ham Common boasted its squad, in which our coachman and a footman figured. And they had their inspections and field-days, with other corps; and we were all very proud, when they returned from one of these with laurel in their caps.'*

Gordon Forbes, the eldest son of General Forbes who lived at Gordon House, moved here when his father died in 1870. He fathered 13 children, 8 of them were born at Forbes House. Sadly, the three youngest boys Charles aged 4, Urquhart aged 2 and Lushington aged 1 all died on the same day in November 1835 from measles and were buried in the family vault at St Peter's. Gordon had served with the East India Company in India as a Civil Servant for over 20 years and on his return to Ham was active in local affairs, associated with the National Orphan Home across the Common as well as the building of St Andrew's Church.

After the death of Gordon Forbes, the house was purchased in 1872 by Harry Warren Scott and his wife Caroline Louisa. Cecilia Nina Cavendish-Bentinck was the eldest daughter of Mrs Scott's first marriage and it was she who married Claude George Bowes-Lyon, Lord Glamis, later Earl of Strathmore in 1881 at St Peter's Church. They had 10 children including Lady Elizabeth Bowes-Lyon, the late Queen Mother who used to come and stay with her grandmother at Forbes House. Elizabeth's older sister Violet Hyacinth was only 11 when she died, whilst staying with her grandmother, of diptheria. The little girl was buried at St Andrew's. Mrs Scott was also the aunt of the famous literary hostess Lady Ottoline Morell and lived at Forbes House until her death in 1918.

In 1935 Mrs Winifred Buckley bought the house and decided to pull it down. The architect Oswald P Milne rebuilt it for her as a neo-Georgian house. In 1949 the widow of Sir George Dance, theatrical manager and author, purchased the freehold and soon sold it on to the Surrey County Council who converted the building into an old people's home. When this closed in 1992, the house was bought by John Beckwith, a director of the London & Edinburgh Trust, and demolished to make way for the present neo-classical building designed by Julian Bicknell and built as a family home which was completed in 1998.

The classically elegant Langham House was built in about 1709. Between 1780 and 1790 it was occupied by the Marquess of Tweeddale and in 1851 it was the home of Charles Edgeworth, half-brother of the Irish author Maria Edgeworth. Active in parish affairs, he was also, along with his neighbour at Forbes House, Gordon Forbes, involved with the management of the National Orphan Home on the other side of the Common.

Admiral of the Fleet Sir John Fisher,
1st Baron of Kilverstone 1841–1920.
©*National Maritime Museum, Greenwich*

Above: Langham House

Opposite: the current Forbes House

Admiral of the Fleet Sir John ('Jacky') Fisher, who was First Sea Lord from 1904 to 1910, lived here. According to the Royal Navy he was '*an outstanding innovator and administrator responsible for wide ranging reforms which transformed the navy of the Victorian age into a military machine capable of maintaining Britain's naval supremacy in the First World War*'. Fisher joined the Royal Navy at the age of 13 in 1854. His first ship was HMS *Victory*, Nelson's flagship at the Battle of Trafalgar. He returned as First Sea Lord for a brief spell in the First World War but resigned after disagreements with the First Lord of the Admiralty, Winston Churchill.

In 1937 Langham House was the home of Air Vice-Marshal Sir Philip Game, air force officer, Governor of New South Wales from 1930 to 1935, and Commissioner of the Metropolitan Police during the Second World War. Sir Lyonel Tollemache and his bachelor son Sir Cecil moved here in 1949 when the Ham House estate was sold after Ham House was transferred to the National Trust.

In 1955 the property was sold and converted into flats. The rear garden was sold separately and Langham House Close was constructed on its site. Designed by Sir James Stirling (1926–92), one of the most important and influential British architects of his generation, and James Gowan for the Manousso Group of companies, this development comprises 30 two- and three-storey flats. A landmark in the emerging style of the late 1950s in England, their design has been described as *'uncompromisingly brutalist'*. They were listed Grade II* in 2006. Langham Cottage, behind the high wall next door, was originally the coach house to Langham House. It was completely rebuilt in 1974.

In the late 18th century a house with a large garden stood between what is now Lawrence Hall and Langham House. In about 1774 it was leased to the Hon George Hobart (1731–1804) as a country villa, for about 27 years. The house became known as 'Sans Souci' after a villa at the famous summer palace at Potsdam, outside Berlin, built in the mid eighteenth century by the King of Prussia, Frederick the Great and now a World Heritage Site. The house was eventually demolished in about 1830.

George Hobart was the elder of two sons of John Hobart (1693–1756), the 1st Earl of Buckinghamshire, by his second marriage in 1728 to Elizabeth Bristow. One of George's father's sisters was Henrietta Hobart, Countess of Suffolk, the mistress of George II and the owner of Marble Hill in Twickenham. George was the manager for a time of the opera at the King's Theatre in the Haymarket. In 1757 he married Albinia Bertie, daughter of Lord Vere Bertie. He inherited the family seat in Nocton in Lincolnshire in 1766 and became the 3rd Earl of Buckinghamshire in 1793 on the death of his half-brother, John.

Albinia eclipsed her husband as a public figure, and leading a separate life, became well known for her lavish assemblies and amateur dramatic performances which were so popular in the second half of the 18th century. They usually featured herself and her daughters, and were often staged at Nocton Hall and from the early 1780s at their 'Villa', Sans Souci on Ham Common. She also performed at the Richmond Theatre. Horace Walpole often mentions the performances at Ham in his letters and also described 'Sans Souci' wittily in July 1781 as *'her hut on Ham Common, where she has built two large rooms of timber under a cabbage'*. Mrs Hobart seemed to be an indefatigable performer. Although a 'woman of fashion', she was the butt of many caricatures of the day on account of her exceptionally buxom figure, but this did not seem to deter her from taking the parts of young heroines in her plays. The performances were attended with enthusiasm by fashionable people from far afield, including the Prince of Wales, the son of George III.

Above: Sir Philip Game, Commissioner of the Metropolitan Police 1935–1945, in ceremonial dress

Below: Grade II* listed flats in Langham House Close, built in the mid 50's

In 1791 Walpole wrote again about Mrs Hobart and Sans Souci: *'Mrs Hobart announced a rural breakfast at Sans Souci last Saturday; nothing being so pastoral as a fat grandmother in a row of houses on Ham Common.'*

George Hobart's younger brother, the Hon Henry Hobart MP, lived at Ivy Hall, otherwise known as *Mr Hobart's House* and now the Hobart Hotel, on the Petersham Road in Richmond. The Duke of Clarence also lived at Ivy Hall for a few months in 1789 (see page 82).

Henry was MP for Norwich from 1786; he played a major role in local ecclesiastical and civil affairs and laid the foundation stone for Richmond Bridge in 1774. He married Ann Margaret Bristow, whose aunt Rebecca and sister Sophia lived at Reston Lodge in Petersham. They were buried at St Peter's in 1775 and 1778.

A satirical, hand-coloured etching (right) of Mrs Hobart dated 1784. She sits stiffly in an opera-box in profile to the left, together with another equally buxom lady. The hair of both is elaborately dressed and surmounted by an erection of feathers, flowers and ribbons. Both have rather grim expressions
©*Trustees of the British Museum*

Here she is depicted (above) in another satirical print, dated 1784, entitled Ham Common Theatre. The proscenium of a small theatre is suggested by an archway over which is the accustomed motto, forming the title, 'Veluti in speculum' (As in a mirror). On the front of the stage, to the left, is a very fat lady identified as Mrs Hobart, with the inscription:
Fore Gad that Caecilia's a charming young Woman!
Were you Miss Larolles at the Play at Ham-Common?

This epilogue to one of the plays was written for Mrs Peter Hobart by Miles Peter Andrews, the playwright, and mimics the typical conversation between characters from Fanny Burney's recently published novel 'Cecilia, or Memoirs of an Heiress'. It goes on to say:
Oh yes, to be sure, you can't think how delightful,
The men were so bad, and the women so frightful,
Such a crowd, so much to eat, and so little to drink,
The time pass'd so pleasantly on, you can't think......
©*Trustees of the British Museum*

A Side Box at the Opera.
Pub March. 15, 1792 by S W Fores Nº 3 Piccadilly.

The Cassel Hospital, a late 18th century Grade II listed building, was formerly known as Morgan House, one of the residences of John Minter Morgan (1782–1854), the wealthy son of a wholesale stationer of Ludgate Hill. An Anglican, socialist writer and philanthropist, Morgan was a campaigner for universal free education and advocated 'self-supporting' villages under the guidance of the established church. He bought the house and grounds in 1835. It was he who also bought and founded the National Orphan Home on the other side of Ham Common in 1848 (see South Lodge page 60). He was buried at St Andrew's on 3 January 1855.

Robert Philippe, Duc de Chartres, lived here from 1863 until 1871 and it was he who added the wings to the house. Married to his cousin the Princesse d'Orléans, and a grandson of Louis Philippe, King of France from 1830 to 1848, he was exiled with him in 1848.

Morgan House became West Heath in 1879, when it was a school for young ladies. In 1930 the Lawrence Memorial Hall attached to the building was built in honour of one of the schoolmistresses, Miss Emma Lawrence. The school moved to Sevenoaks, Kent at this time and later became famous when Diana Princess of Wales was a pupil.

It then became a hotel, the Lawrence Hall Hotel, until the Cassel Foundation bought the estate in 1947. The Cassel Hospital was previously at Penshurst in Kent and then during the Second World War it moved to Stoke-on-Trent. Originally a hospital for psychological casualties of the First World War it was founded and endowed by the millionaire philanthropist Sir Ernest Cassel, the son of a Cologne banker. Born in 1852, he came to England, penniless, at the age of 16. He had a natural business sense and became a successful merchant banker and capitalist. He was knighted by Queen Victoria in 1889 and became a Privy Councillor in 1902. Edwina Ashley, the late Countess Mountbatten, was his granddaughter. Now the hospital offers a specialist service treating adults, young people and families with intractable personality and family disorders; it is run by the NHS and offers residential, day and outreach services. Planning permission was given recently to build flats in the hospital grounds, alongside and to the south of the main building and facing the Common; the new building is called Morgan House.

The Gate House Garden at the corner of Ham Common was established in 1983 by the Ham Amenities Group, following their purchase of this small patch of land which had previously been an untidy eyesore. They installed a water supply for the gardeners and seats for passers-by, and the garden is now an award-winning local asset, full of flowers in the summer.

On the east side of the Upper Ham Road is Parkleys, built in 1953–56 and arguably the most successful of the major 20th century building developments in the district. It was built on land formerly part of Ham Farm Nursery, together with the grounds of The Elms, later known as Cairn House, which was demolished at the start of the project. This was where the annual flower show and Ham Horticultural shows were held in the early 1900s.

The largest of Sir Eric Lyons's Span estates, Parkleys comprises 169 flats and six shops in two- and three-storey blocks, well designed with pleasantly scaled enclosed courts and notable landscaping in keeping

with the buildings; each group is named after a poet.
Lyons and his associated firm Span are renowned for
their post-war, high-density and controlled housing
schemes that fostered the community spirit in a shared
landscape. Some of the magnificent trees from the days
of The Elms garden were carefully incorporated in the
design and still survive. Thirteen houses on individual
plots along Ham Farm Road were also developed as
part of the estate in 1955/6. An innovative resident-
controlled company was established to manage the
maintenance and alteration of the flats and the
surrounding landscaping. The estate received Grade
II* listed status in 2007.

Opposite: An early 1900 photo of Cassel Hospital
Reproduced by kind permission of Sir David
Williams and as it is today

Above: Lawrence Hall

Below: : Sir Ernest Cassel,
a watercolour by Anders Zorn, 1886

The Gate House, so called because there was a gate across the road nearby to stop animals straying off the common, was once an almshouse. It still stands, opposite Parkleys on Ham Parade, and is now part of the group of buildings occupied by the solicitors Dixon Roe. The inscription on the front of the building reads *'Erected by the inhabitants of Ham and Hatch in 1771'.* Mrs Sarah 'Grannie' Morffew, the daughter of a charcoal burner, lived here for 40 years. Apparently very fond of snuff, she died in 1892 at the age of 105, according to her death certificate of senility and exhaustion, and is buried in St Andrew's churchyard.

What is now the florist, Pick of the Bunch, next to the cricket pavilion on the Upper Ham Road, used to be a gentlemen's hairdressers in the 1960s. The proprietor was known to every small boy in the area as Chopper Harris. It was later taken over by John Vickery and operated as a newsagent's business in tandem with the main shop and Post Office on Ham Parade. The small premises next door which is now the Dog and Groom was rented by Fred Burgess for his tailoring business until he retired in 1957; for a short time it was also a surveyor's office.

Fox House was built on common land in about 1777 by John Denton, a carpenter. It was once known as Chestnut Cottage and also the Rosery. The land was farmed by the copyholder (a tenant of the manor whose title deed was a 'copy' of the appropriate entry in the Lord's manor court roll; transfers of copyhold, whether by sale or inheritance, could only be made with the court's agreement and on payment of a fee). The house has since been much extended.

Ham Common Woods, an area of over 74 acres that stretches from the Upper Ham Road to Ham Gate, is also part of the Common. Now densely wooded, 50 years ago this area was more open and Silvia Greenwood, who came from a family which settled in Ham in about 1830, remembered how there used to be a common-keeper's hut on the south side of Ham Gate Avenue and how before the Second World War nightingales could be heard singing here. It has become one of the ongoing battles of the Ham and Petersham Association to ensure that these woods are once again maintained and that a more open aspect is restored for the enjoyment of walkers and residents alike.

It would take the brush of an artist or the pen of a writer to capture and do justice to the charm and quiet peaceful beauty of Ham as it was in 1922 when I came to live here. The lovely common, surrounded by fine trees of elm and lime with twin rows of stately elms across it was a picture in itself, but added to this was the country atmosphere of rooks cawing in the trees, cows quietly grazing and drinking from the pond where ducks swam and bull frogs croaked at night It was indeed hard to believe that we were only twelve miles from London.

'Reminiscences' by Marjorie Lansdale

Sir Eric Lyons OBE (1912–1980), one of the most respected British housing architects of the 20th century
John Donat/RIBA Library Photographs Collection

Above: 'Grannie' Morffew sitting outside the Gate House on the Upper Ham Road in 1891 *Reproduced by kind permission of Sir David Williams* and how it looks today

Below: Chopper Harris the barber's and Vickery's newsagents in the 1960s. Next to it, the shops today

Right: The statue of a naked woman with a bird on a nest at Parkleys was sculpted by Keith Godwin. It is said to represent 'home-making' and was unveiled by the architect Sir Hugh Casson in the 1960s

In the late 19th century James Walker leased 134 acres of land from the Dysarts at Ham Farm Nursery, the area now south of Ham Farm Road. He was noted not only for growing apples, plums, pears, nectarines and peaches but also for cultivating narcissi and daffodils, as well as tulips, irises, gladioli, lilies, peonies, cyclamens and chrysanthemums, many under glass at his large nursery. Miss Lansdale mentions in her recollections that the family still had a large fruit farm and orchard here as late as the 1930s.

St Andrew's Church on Church Road was built in 1831 in the neo-Gothic style on common land provided reluctantly by the Lady of the Manor, Louisa, 7th Countess of Dysart. It was paid for by public subscription. Until that time, Ham had no church of its own. The building, by the architect Edward Lapidge, was of London stock brick with Bath stone lancet windows and portals. The original church with its two turrets was a rectangular building the size of the present nave, and was known locally as the *'Chapel on the Common'*.

Church Road was laid out at this time and stretched from the new church to the main road; it was later extended to Latchmere House and then to the Ham Gate of Richmond Park. By 1857 the church was considered inadequate for the needs of the growing parish, and a south wing (now known as the Lady Chapel) was added.

In 1896 the famous Victorian architect G F Bodley designed a splendid Chancel, decorated in a blaze of colour. A Vestry room was added to the church, and further additions including the Chancel were completed in the early 1900s. The East Window, depicting the Crucifixion, was designed by Ninian Comper (later Sir Ninian) in 1900 and given by Mrs Scott of Forbes House on Ham Common.

The Revd Arthur Stanley Vaughan Blunt was vicar from 1898 to 1906. He was married to Hilda Violet Master, the youngest of four daughters of Henry and Gertrude Master of Montrose House. The Blunt's son Anthony was the fourth man in the 1950s Russian spy scandal. In the churchyard is the grave of the war hero and Scottish rugby international Group Captain Sir Louis Greig. He was a naval surgeon (later transferring to the RAF), a friend of King George VI and for a time his equerry. It is said that Greig's influence helped guide the young Prince Albert, a shy stammering schoolboy, to become one of the most respected of our constitutional monarchs. He was appointed deputy Ranger of Richmond Park in 1932 and in 1937 became the chairman of the All England Croquet and Lawn Tennis Club at Wimbledon. He lived at Thatched House Lodge in Richmond Park.

The War Memorial in the churchyard, made of Red Corsehill stone, was built in 1920 to commemorate the forty dead of the First World War who lived in and around Ham.

The early Victorian Latchmere House was originally a residential home. In the late 1800s it was the home of Joshua Field (1829–1904), JP for London and Surrey and Deputy Lieutenant for Surrey. A mechanical engineer, he was one of the partners of Maudsley and Field of Lambeth, a famous firm of Victorian engineers founded by his father of the same name, which built the engines for Brunel's steamship *Great Britain*. He and his wife Emma Jessie had 14 children, four of whom are buried in St Andrew's churchyard with their parents.

During the First World War the army used Latchmere to billet soldiers; later it became a convalescent home for shell-shocked officers. In the Second World War it was used by MI5 as Britain's secret interrogation centre for captured enemy spies, known as 'Camp 020'. Some 480 spies passed through the Camp. Declassified papers released to the Public Record Office in 1999 show that MI5 officers used specific questioning techniques and investigative skills designed to create an aura of 'remorseless efficiency', and to get their prisoners to talk without resorting to the sadistic means attributed to their Nazi opponents. Although the conditions were sometimes severe, no physical

Opposite: St Andrew's from the south east showing the War Memorial which was built in 1920

Above: The church as it is today

Right: An early 1900s photo of the same view
Reproduced by kind permission of Sir David Williams

violence or curtailment of food rations was ever applied. The building was modified to prevent communication between inmates and to glean as much information as possible from them during their short stay at the facility. It is said that listening devices were placed in the cells and that pipes were buried within the masonry to prevent prisoners tapping Morse code to one another. Camp 020 also played a key role in the Security Service's now legendary 'Double Cross System', whereby German spies were sometimes turned into double agents. The camp also provided useful information for Allied code breakers at Bletchley Park and, in the closing stages of the war, it was responsible for 'breaking' several captured Nazi leaders, some of whom were then successfully tried by the Allies at Nuremberg.

Lt Colonel Robin Stephens, known as 'Tin Eye' because of his thick monocle, was the commander of this wartime prison. By all accounts he was a formidable character who had an extraordinary ability to break even the hardest of spies. *'Never strike a man'* wrote Stephens in his instructions for interrogators. *'In the first place it is an act of cowardice. In the second place, it is not intelligent. A prisoner will lie to avoid further punishment and everything he says thereafter will be based on a false premise.'*

The prison service took over the former military site in 1948. Over the years HMP Latchmere House has changed its role in the prison service and it has been used successively as a young offender institution, a remand centre and a deportees' prison. It became an adult male resettlement prison in 1991. Although the perimeter is fenced, it is a semi-open prison and prisoners who arrive here are approaching the end of their sentences.

Latchmere Lodge is now known as Wilmer House. In 1841 it was the home of the Revd Thomas Hore, and was also owned for a time by Joshua Field who lived at Latchmere House, next door. It was burnt down in the early 1930s and subsequently rebuilt.

Park Gate House, adjacent to Ham Gate, is the sole remaining remnant of a large estate called Loanes, most of which, including the principal Loanes House, was enclosed by Charles I in his new Richmond Park. It had belonged to a William Clifton whose executor sold to the King in 1637 for £370. The demolition of Loanes House is noted in the Park accounts for 1637–38, but the name was promptly transferred to a remaining house just outside Ham Gate. In 1699 the Loanes was owned by Sir Thomas Jenner (see Montrose House page 100) and appears to have been a farmhouse; the name of the tenant farmer was James Welbeloved. The Jenner family retained control of the property until 1768, when it was rebuilt. On Sunday 24 July, 1768 Lady Mary Coke (see Sudbrook Park page 112), in her *Letters and Journals, Volume II*, wrote enthusiastically about what is probably the new house that we see today:

'I was quite surprised with a white House just opposite to the great room: 'tis rise upon Ham Common since I was there, & must be, as I told my sister, the work of a Genii, & I believe, a friendly one for it has the appearance of a very Handsome House, & being white is an exceeding pretty object. Sudbrook, tho' an agreeable Place, is rather dull, & the views of this House, as it is at a convenient distance, gives a more cheerful air.'

The distance from Sudbrook Park to Park Gate House is over half a mile and despite the park wall the house would have been clearly visible at the time. Now, sadly, the view is obscured by the trees in Ham Common Woods.

During the 18th century there were several changes of ownership. From 1812, Benjamin Barnard, Sheriff of Surrey and a Cornhill banker lived here with his wife Elizabeth. In 1865 he changed the name from The Loanes to Park Gate House. The census records show a General John Hanbury living here in the late 1800s as well as Lord Charles de la Poer Beresford (see notes).

From 1954 to 1979 it was the home of members of the Vestey family (see notes) and has since been the home of an Arab prince who has made significant changes to the house and grounds.

Ham Gate is one of the six historic gates into Richmond Park dating from the time of its enclosure by Charles I. The lodge was built at the gate in 1742 and in 1758 a ladder-stile was put up at the side which was still in existence in 1850. In 1921 the present wrought-iron gates were substituted for the old wooden ones.

Ormeley Lodge (above) on Ham Gate Avenue was built in about 1715 by Thomas Hamond, one of the younger sons of Leonard Hamond of Teddington, at about the same time as the Duke of Argyll was building Sudbrook Park. The fine entrance gate, seen from Ham Gate Avenue, has an elaborate overthrow in wrought iron; this extends along the front of the house between brick piers crowned with terminal vases. Through the gates, the notable front raised doorway has Corinthian pilasters and an ornamental frieze carved with cherubs' heads. Pevsner describes the house as 'exquisite' and it certainly is one of the most beautiful houses in Ham.

In 1763 the Lodge was bought, as a country retreat, by the Hon Charles Townshend (1725–1767), the enigmatic statesman who became Lord of the Admiralty and later Chancellor of the Exchequer. Townshend was married to Lady Caroline Campbell, Lady Greenwich. They moved to Sudbrook Park on the death of the Dowager Duchess of Argyll in 1767. It was here that Townshend suddenly died at the age of 42 from a 'putrid fever'. Walpole, expressing the shock and loss to the political scene of the day, wrote: *'That first eloquence of the world is dumb.'*

It has been said that the future King George IV, when the Prince of Wales, and Maria Fitzherbert spent their honeymoon at Ormeley Lodge in December 1785, after their marriage, but this has never been substantiated.

From 1814 to 1819 Ormeley Lodge was one of the homes of the Scottish politician Sir John Sinclair MP (1754–1835), of Ulbster, Caithness. He was President of the Board of Agriculture. His fourth daughter was Catherine Sinclair (1800–1864) who was her father's secretary from the age of 14 until his death and went on to write some 28 works: children's books, including *Holiday House* (1839), light romances and travel guides. She became renowned for her charitable works and is remembered by a grand Gothic memorial in Edinburgh's Queen Street.

In 1893 the house became the home of Charles Hanbury-Tracy, 4th Lord Sudeley of Toddington, and his wife Ada, niece of the 8th Earl of Dysart and granddaughter of Gordon Forbes of Forbes House; it seems likely that the house was bought for them by the Dysarts. Lord Sudeley had joined the Navy at the age of 14, and saw action in the Crimean War.

He went into Parliament, representing the Montgomery Boroughs until he inherited the peerage in 1877. He held office under Gladstone's administration in the early 1880s and represented the Board of Trade and Office of Works on the Front Bench in the House of Lords. He also attended Queen Victoria as Lord-in-Waiting. In considering which Lords-in-Waiting should accompany her to Osborne House in the Isle of Wight, it is said that Queen Victoria exclaimed *'Not Lord Sudeley, he is so dull.'* However on hearing the news of his bankruptcy the old Queen is reported to have wept.

He became bankrupt in 1900 and much of Ada's fortune (which came from her father's brother Algernon Tollemache, and which she had entrusted to her husband) was lost. He had to leave the House of Lords, but was able to return after the discharge for which he successfully applied in 1903. Thereafter he used his seat in the House of Lords to advocate official guide lecturers for our national museums and picture galleries and was largely instrumental in securing their appointment. When Lord Sudeley died in 1922 Lady Sudeley moved to Reston Lodge in Petersham; she died in 1928.

Opposite: Ormeley Lodge

Above: Charles Douglas Richard Hanbury-Tracy, 4th Baron Sudeley, a pencil drawing by Frederick Sargent c.1880 ©*National Portrait Gallery*

The fine wrought iron overthrow to the front gate of Ormeley Lodge

An early 1900s postcard of Ham Gate Avenue with Ormeley Lodge on the left. *Reproduced by kind permission of Sir David Williams.* Note the young sycamore trees lining the road. Sadly, many of these splendid trees are now suffering from 'sooty bark' disease

Opposite: An early pen-and-ink drawing by Richard Cooper II (1740–1814) of the landscape around Ormeley Lodge shortly after the house was built by Thomas Hamond
©*The Trustees of the British Museum*

Below: The Ham Obelisk at the corner of Ham Gate Avenue and the Upper Ham Road and two views of Ham Gate Avenue looking towards Ham Gate

Felix Charles Hubert Hanbury-Tracy, their youngest son, a lieutenant in the Scots Guards, was killed in action in France in 1914 aged 32. As well as being commemorated on the Ploegsteert Memorial in Belgium as he has no known grave, there is also a memorial to him in St Andrew's Church. Their second son Major Algernon Henry Charles Hanbury-Tracy (CMG) of the Royal Horse Guards died in England form wounds sustained in France in the First World War, aged 44 a year after his brother. He is buried at St Peter's. Both brothers also lost a son in the Second World War.

Ormeley Lodge was purchased in the 1949 Ham and Petersham estate auction by Ronald A Lee, an antique dealer, who lived there for some eight years. In 1954 he held an important loan exhibition of antiques in the house, 'Masterpieces of British Art and Craftmanship'. Ronald Lee sold the house to the Earl and Countess of Westmoreland, and in 1964 they in turn sold it to Lord and Lady Howard de Walden.

The Ham Obelisk which stands on the corner of Ham Gate Avenue and the Upper Ham Road is believed to have been one of a pair of lamp standards that stood outside Ormeley Lodge in the 1870s when the 4th Lord Sudeley lived there.

Hatch Court was the manor house of the Hatch part of Kingston Canbury which stood somewhere to the north and east of where Ormeley Lodge stands today. Its exact situation is unknown but its 17 acres of land today form the southern end of the Richmond golf course in Sudbrook Park. The earliest reference we have to Hatch Court is in a survey of Kingston Canbury manor dated 1562 in which it is stated that Alice Wells holds 'the whole manor of Hatch with all arable lands, closes and cottages thereto pertaining called Hatch Court'. In 1715 the Duke of Argyll bought the estate for use as a hunting lodge, at the same time as building was being started on Sudbrook Park nearby. Soon after, in 1721, Hatch Court was burnt down and it was never rebuilt.

Right: Sudbrook Lodge

Below: The frontispiece of Beverley Nichols'
most famous book *Down the Garden Path*, still in
print some 70 years after its first publication in
1932, and a photograph of the author with his
favourite cat taken by Godfrey Argent
©*National Portrait Gallery*

Opposite: Sudbrook Cottages and the famous
garden which was created by Beverley Nichols

Sudbrook Lodge, the tall brick house across the main road from the New Inn, was rebuilt in about 1680 by Elizabeth Wigington, a widow and the only daughter of Thomas Hunt, a London timber merchant. At about the same time, in 1679, she sold 13 acres of pasture land known as Hatching Mere, lying between Ham Common and Petersham Fields, to the Duchess of Lauderdale.

There is a local story that Nell Gwynn, mistress of Charles II, was living at Sudbrook Lodge at the time of the birth of their illegitimate son Charles Beauclerk, who was later created Duke of St Albans. However, he was born in 1670, before Sudbrook Lodge was built. Another story about the house is that in the 1950s the Revd Canon Beard, vicar of St Andrew's at the time, was apparently called in to exorcise a poltergeist after some workmen discovered a hidden priest's hole in the house. There was a local rumour at the time that the poltergeist promptly moved to the Vicarage.

Notable occupants of Sudbrook Lodge include the author Sir Compton Mackenzie, who lived here for a short time in 1944, and Lady Duckham, the widow of Sir Arthur Duckham, also an author, who bought the house in 1956. The Old Coach House, next door, used to be the Lodge's coach house and stables until 1957 when it was converted into a separate dwelling.

Mrs Wigington's descendants also sold the land which is today known as Sudbrook Gardens to the Duke of Argyll, and it became the kitchen gardens of Sudbrook Park. They extended along the rear of the cottages on Ham Gate Avenue, an attractive and externally unspoilt group of terraced houses with shallow slate hipped roofs on narrow plots with distinctive trellis porches. One of these, Sudbrook Cottage, was the home of (John) Beverley Nichols (1898–1983), an accomplished gardener, musician, author and lyricist, who wrote extensively for the London revues of the 1930s. Osbert Sitwell described him in the 1920s as *'the original bright young thing'*. He was President of the forerunner of the Ham and Petersham Association in 1959.

The New Inn stands at the north-east corner of the open area of Ham Common. There has been an inn on this site at least since 1675. It was named the White Hart before it was rebuilt in 1756 as the building we see today and subsequently called the New Inn. In about 1780 the name of the inn was changed again to the Hobart Arms, probably after the Hon George Hobart who lived on the other side of the Common, but by about 1822 its name had reverted to the New Inn. It was here that the Ham Vestry meetings took place before St Andrew's Church was built. Close to the inn there used to be a gate across the main road to stop animals straying off the common, the counterpart of the one by the Gate House opposite Parkleys.

Stafford Cottages next door to the New Inn is one of the oldest buildings in Ham, dating back to the beginning of the 17th century. It was not until 1799 that the building was divided into three dwellings, which in 1851 were occupied by two gardeners, a carpenter and their families. It is now a single dwelling again.

Opposite, above: The New Inn public house and Sudbrook Lodge c.1907 photographed by W S Campbell. *Rural Nooks Around London* by Charles G Harper, Chapman and Hall Ltd, 1907

Opposite right: Stafford Cottages

This page: Early 1900s postcards of the view along the Upper Ham Road towards the New Inn public house *by kind permission of Sir David Williams.*

Right: A group of men stand proudly beside their penny-farthings outside the public house; above: note the cow grazing on the side of the road and the open aspect behind the row of lime trees to what is now part of Ham Common Woods and the New Inn and the Upper Ham Road today

The site of the present-day South Lodge on fashionable Ham Common was an unlikely setting for an alternative community dedicated to an experiment designed to change the world and to create a New Eden. Founded in 1838 by the theosopher and mystic James Pierrepont Greaves (1777–1842), Alcott House, also known as the Concordium, was both a progressive school and a working community composed of devoted followers (ideally celibate) of Greaves, and the unfortunate who could find nowhere else to live and had to be grateful for what they received. The phrase 'New Age' was first used by the community for one of their publications and they eagerly embraced all new fads like mesmerism, phrenology, vegetarianism and hydrotherapy. Many of the radically unorthodox of the day visited them at Alcott House, including Amos Bronson Alcott, the American Transcendentalist philosopher and educator, who stayed with the community in 1842.

The community struggled on for ten years, with about thirty members at its peak, subscribing to the belief that reform must come not from material goods or social organisation but spiritually from within. It was an austere environment. Meals were preferably uncooked, consisting mainly of whole wheat bread and added raisins, fruit and cold vegetables which they grew themselves in the 4-acre grounds. To create the necessary harmony within and without, they eschewed alcohol, meat, salt and spices as too exciting.

Opposite: The National Orphan Home, Ham Common, from The Graphic, 11 July 1874. As well as instruction in reading, writing, grammar and simple arithmetic, the girls also received training that would help them find suitable positions as domestic servants when they left at the age of 15

A coloured engraving of South Lodge in 1868. Note the attractive boundary wall of which sadly only the base remains today

1. View of the Home from the Common.—2. Scrubbing the Dormitories.—3. In the Laundry.—4. In the Playground.

A VISIT TO THE NATIONAL ORPHAN HOME, HAM COMMON, SURREY

The regime was quasi-monastic, with bells ringing to announce the various stages in the day, starting each morning at about 5 o'clock. The men grew long beards and wore loose clothes and sandals, whilst the women discarded the conventional corset. The school catered for the children of radical sympathisers, generally from outside the community. A diverse curriculum was followed, depending on who was resident at the time and what they could manage to teach; the school was, however, based on the Pestalozzian principle of the child's innate goodness.

The gifted young teacher in the early years was Henry Gardiner Wright. A remarkable account of two of his lessons, based on an inductive dialogue with the small children, survives. William Oldham was the administrative head. When Bronson Alcott, funded by Ralph Waldo Emerson, came in the summer of 1842 to visit the community bearing his name, he found that Greaves had recently died but the American was excited by his welcome. He found Wright possessing 'the rare art of reaching men and women' and wrote home to his brother 'Ham is home to me'. When he returned to New England Alcott took Wright and another Greaves follower, Charles Lane, with him in the hope of setting up the Ham community in America.

Alcott and his family with Lane did establish a community, Fruitlands, on a 50-acre site near Harvard, Massachusetts, but it lasted barely six months. Louisa M Alcott was eleven when she witnessed her father's experiment in creating a New Eden and she later wrote a subversive short story *Transcendental Wild Oats* to show what it was really like.

The quack remedy called Hydropathy, invented in Germany by Vincent Preissnitz, was introduced to England by his associate C von Schlemmer who came with his sons to the Concordium in 1841 to learn English, and instructed Wright's wife Elizabeth in the techniques. Hydropathy was a fashionable cure-all in Victorian times, albeit with many sceptics. The community would bathe in cold water, drink pints of water and wrap themselves in wet sheets with the aim of stimulating the circulation and drawing the blood supply from the affected parts. All manner of ailments were said to be successfully treated by this natural remedy when conventional medicine of the time achieved little. In 1842 Greaves himself became a patient but in fact died from a severe hernia. He was buried at St Andrew's. As the water cure became more popular, new institutions were founded in England, including for a time one at Sudbrook Park (see page 112).

Opposite: Early 1900s photo of South Lodge with
girls from the National Orphan Home sitting on
the Common in front. The building is of the
Italianate style with a notable crowning cupola
*Reproduced by kind permission of Sir David
Williams*

This page: South Lodge today

In 1848 the 3-acre site with two small houses and out-
buildings previously occupied by the Concordium was
bought from the Dysarts by John Minter Morgan (see
Cassel Hospital, page 44) to provide a home for girls
left orphaned and destitute by the current serious
outbreak of cholera. The management committee of
the home resolved to build a larger house for orphans
from subscription and in 1862 the central part of South
Lodge that we see today was built, the wings and the
front wall being added in 1868 and 1872. It became
known as the National Orphan Home and the charity
offered accommodation for 120 girls, many of them
orphans from the Crimean War. The Home was in
existence for more than 50 years, closing eventually in
1922.

In the Second World War South Lodge became a
Community Centre run by the Women's Voluntary
Service where they served the healthy Woolton Pie
(named after Lord Woolton, the wartime Minister of
Food). Soon after the war South Lodge was converted
into flats and the garden was sold off separately for the
development of Bishop's Close.

The part stucco-faced Hardwicke House was built in 1688 for the English dietary reformer Thomas Tryon (1634–1703) as his country residence; he had bought some of the land from the son of Elizabeth Wigington at Sudbrook Lodge. Born in Bibury, near Gloucester, he tended a flock of his father's sheep from the age of 11. Having an earnest desire to travel, at 18 he made his way to London and became an apprentice to a 'castor-maker' (a castor was a fur hat). He developed an interest in dietetics, was against animal cruelty and strongly recommended a vegetarian diet, abstinence from tobacco and alcohol and indeed from all luxuries; he went on to write more than 20 works about health and diet. Many of his books became widely read, particularly *A Treatise of English Herbs and The Way to Health, Long Life and Happiness.*

Between Hardwicke House and St Michael's Convent, just where Martingales Close now starts, there used to be a 'little cottage at Ham Common' that was owned by General William Eden. He died in 1851 aged 84 and was buried at St Andrew's; it is said that his favourite charger was buried under a mound on Ham Common. His two cousins Fanny and Emily Eden established a household here for a time and it was here that Emily wrote her first novel *The Semi-Attached Couple.* Fanny and Emily were sisters of George Eden, Lord Auckland. He was appointed Governor-General of India and his sisters accompanied him to Calcutta where they made an official tour of north-western India in 1837. Emily wrote letters home recording all her impressions in an amusing, vivacious and ironic fashion, describing not only the mundane but also state travel in the company of no less than 12,000 people, with hundreds of animals and wagons, sometimes on camel-back, sometimes in palanquins or in elephant howdahs, over a period of two years. These letters formed the basis for her best-known book *Up the Country,* published in 1866. She was also a talented amateur painter and some of her accomplished lithographs were published in *Portraits of the People and Princes of India* in 1844.

Above: Thomas Tryon c.1700 *'Plant not the Flowers of Indulgence. Sow Compassion and Justice in their place.'*

Below: Hardwicke House

Opposite: St Michael's Convent

Emily Eden, a watercolour and pencil drawing by Simon Jacques Rochard, 1835
©*National Portrait Gallery*

St Michael's Convent (originally Orford House or Orford Hall) and Avenue Lodge next door were built probably at the same time in about 1730 for William Genew, the son of another William Genew, the owner of Ham Manor House. In 1871 Orford House became a girls' school run by Hannah Fitt from Norfolk, and by 1882 it was the home of three spinster Beckford sisters, originally from Bath, and their numerous servants including a coachman. In the early 1900s the two younger Hornby sisters, who had also lived at the Manor House in Ham, came to live here. Both the Beckford and Hornby sisters were active in local affairs.

In 1949 Orford House was bought by the international Anglican Community of the Sisters of the Church, an order founded in 1870, to become the Mother House and Novitiate of the order. The main central block of the house was enlarged in the late 1950s to include two new wings and a chapel which was dedicated in 1956. The Sisters are involved in pastoral work and priestly ministry with, in their words, a particular commitment to hospitality and spiritual accompaniment. The Eucharist is celebrated here on most days, as well as Morning and Evening Prayer and Compline. Today, the

Opposite: A mid 1900s photo of the north of Ham Common with St Anselm's House (number 43) on the left, Boxall Cottages and Avenue Lodge on the right

The two Gate House Lodges today on either side of the Great South Avenue that leads to Ham House

Below: The walled organic vegetable garden of the Community of the Sisters of the Church at St Michael's Convent

Sisters offer space and time for people needing spiritual refreshment and time to just be; and for groups to meet in beautiful and friendly surroundings. There are a range of retreats for quiet prayer and meditation, workshops, days of creativity, lectures and services.

In 1969 Martingales Close was built on land formerly part of the gardens of Hardwicke House, St Michael's Convent and Avenue Lodge. But the Community of the Sisters of the Church, today familiar figures in the area, still have extensive gardens, including a walled organic vegetable garden, which are regularly open to the public in the summer under the National Gardens Scheme.

The Gate House Lodges are a pair of small Jacobean style buildings with Dutch gables probably built at the same time as the Ham Avenues were laid out in about 1679. The lodge on the eastern side was enclosed within the grounds of the next door house, Avenue Lodge, when Lord Dysart purchased it in 1892, so that only the top half can now be seen from the entrance to the avenue over the enclosing wall. This Lodge has retained many of the original features but its twin on the western side was extended in the 1950s.

One of the earliest paintings of Petersham, from
Richmond Hill, attributed to Adriæn van Diest. It
shows several houses in Petersham that existed
in about 1700. The most prominent is the
imposing New Park designed by Matthew
Banckes, later known as the (old) Petersham
Lodge which was destroyed by fire in 1721. It is
not certain if the house with the four chimneys
to the right of the Lodge is the predecessor of
what is now Church House. Directly behind the
spire of St Peter's church is Petersham House,
surmounted by a cupola. On the right is the then
L-shaped Rutland Lodge, and Ham House can be
seen centre right near the river
*The Earl of Rochester's House, New Park,
Richmond, Surrey, c.1700–5. Yale Centre for
British Art, Paul Mellon Collection*

The famous prospect from Richmond Hill, with Petersham Meadows in the foreground, is a rural scene unique today so close to the capital. Beyond the pastoral meadowland with its grazing cows, unchanged for hundreds of years, Petersham sits peacefully within the level floodplain of the river Thames. It is not surprising that the view from Richmond Hill has featured in many famous paintings, notably by J M W Turner (1775–1851), who exhibited his *Richmond Hill on the Prince Regent's Birthday* at the Royal Academy in 1819. The view is protected *'for the use, enjoyment and recreation of the general public'* by the 1902 Richmond, Petersham and Ham Open Spaces Act, which was the result of a public campaign to protect the area from development (see page 9); the Act also transferred the ownership of the meadows from the Dysart estate to the Richmond Corporation. This legal protection of a view by Act of Parliament is thought to be unique.

In 1726 the Swiss traveller and diplomat César de Saussure wrote: *'At the foot of Richmond Hill is the pretty village of Petersham. It is composed of ten or twelve mansions, all having beautiful gardens and belonging to persons of rank. Leaving this village you see two long and wide avenues of trees – close by is Ham, a fine large house belonging to the Earl of Dysart. This residence is on the banks of the Thames and had such fine walks and avenues of trees as to attract all the grand company from Richmond.'*

Above: An 1890 map showing the Petersham section of the proposed borough boundary
Reproduction by kind permission of the Local Studies Library, Richmond

Right: Cows grazing on the Petersham Meadows in summer

Far right: A view of the meadows showing the Petersham Hotel and the Star and Garter Home on the right

In 1998 there was growing local concern about the state of the meadows, which were run down and poorly maintained, and a public meeting was held at the Village Hall in Petersham to discuss what action could be taken. As a result Chris Brasher (see notes), a local resident, set up the Petersham Trust which leased the land from Richmond Council. Its initial aims were to restore and maintain the meadows and ensure that cows graze there for the greater part of the year, with the long-term intention of handing the land over to the National Trust with an endowment. Over the next ten years the Trust successfully restored the land and milking parlour, erected a new barn, raised funds for the endowment and kept cattle grazing on the meadows during the spring and summer months, it being no longer financially viable to run a dairy herd on such a small site.

Petersham Farm in the south-east corner of the meadow was once known as Star Farm Cottages. Several dilapidated farm buildings here were demolished in 2008 to make way for a new development.

There were once tile kilns by the Richmond riverside just outside the Petersham boundary and clay was dug for tile production on the hillside on the other side of the Petersham Road. The tile kilns were closed down in 1767, fortunately leaving the landscape here more rural now than it was 300 years ago. The Earl of Cardigan, later Duke of Montagu, bought the tile kilns and the grounds on the hillside where the clay had been dug, combined them with a large parcel of land from the adjacent Hill Common and converted them all into gardens.

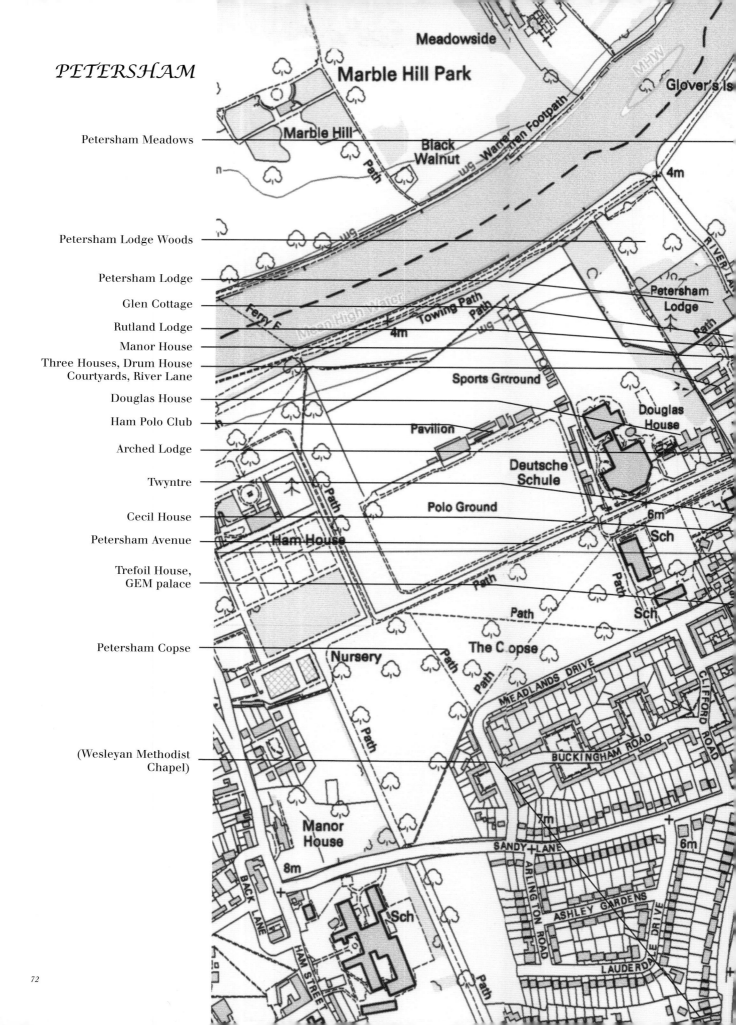

PETERSHAM

Petersham Meadows

Petersham Lodge Woods

Petersham Lodge

Glen Cottage

Rutland Lodge

Manor House

Three Houses, Drum House
Courtyards, River Lane

Douglas House

Ham Polo Club

Arched Lodge

Twyntre

Cecil House

Petersham Avenue

Trefoil House,
GEM palace

Petersham Copse

(Wesleyan Methodist
Chapel)

Meadowside

Marble Hill Park

Glover's Is

Marble Hill

Black
Walnut

Warren Footpath

4m

MHW

River Lane

Petersham
Lodge

Path

Ferry F

Mean High Water

Towing Path

4m

Sports Ground

Douglas
House

Pavilion

Deutsche
Schule

6m

Polo Ground

Sch

Ham House

Path

Path

Sch

Path

Path

The Copse

Path

Path

Nursery

Path

MEADLANDS DRIVE

CLIFFORD ROAD

BUCKINGHAM ROAD

Path

7m

SANDY LANE

6m

Manor
House

8m

BACK LANE

ARLINGTON ROAD

ASHLEY GARDENS

LAUDERDALE DRIVE

HAM STREET

Sch

Path

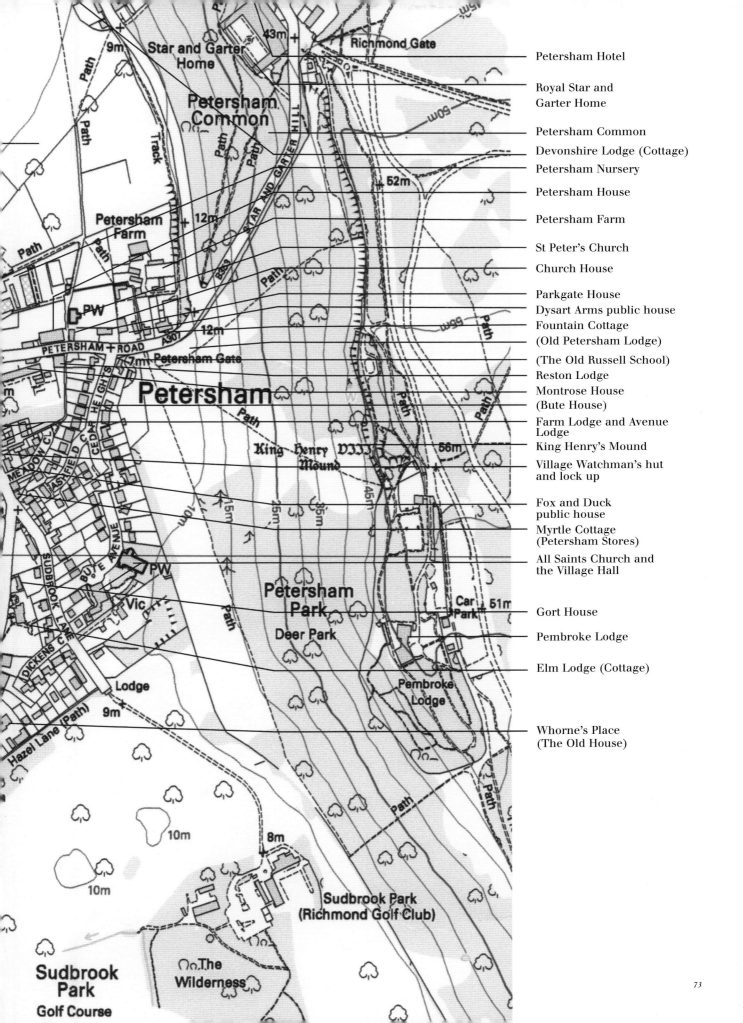

Petersham Hotel

Royal Star and
Garter Home

Petersham Common

Devonshire Lodge (Cottage)

Petersham Nursery

Petersham House

Petersham Farm

St Peter's Church

Church House

Parkgate House

Dysart Arms public house

Fountain Cottage
(Old Petersham Lodge)

(The Old Russell School)

Reston Lodge

Montrose House
(Bute House)

Farm Lodge and Avenue
Lodge

King Henry's Mound

Village Watchman's hut
and lock up

Fox and Duck
public house

Myrtle Cottage
(Petersham Stores)

All Saints Church and
the Village Hall

Gort House

Pembroke Lodge

Elm Lodge (Cottage)

Whorne's Place
(The Old House)

The Duke lived at Montagu House, by the riverbank north of the meadows. His daughter Lady Elizabeth eventually inherited this house, which became known as Buccleuch House following her marriage in 1767 to Sir Henry Scott, 3rd Duke of Buccleuch.

In the 1670s, a chalybeate spring was discovered on the Richmond side of the tile kilns. The water was claimed to have medicinal properties similar to the Epsom waters which were then already famous. To exploit this natural resource new buildings were erected, concerts and dancing were advertised, and Richmond Wells became a successful enterprise attracting large numbers of fashionable people from the capital.

Devonshire Cottage, later known as Devonshire Lodge, once stood by the Petersham Road on the north-eastern edge of Petersham Meadows. In the 1780s, after the death of her second husband, it was the home of the painter Lady Diana Beauclerk, 'Lady Di' (see notes), and it was later occupied by Elizabeth, Duchess of Devonshire. A Cedar of Lebanon is all that remains, together with a stone plaque recording the name of the house in the wall by the gate that leads to Buccleuch Gardens. The stone was laid by the Hon Mrs Caroline Lamb who lived here for almost 30 years until the 1860s. She let the house during the summer months to Mary and Agnes Berry, the socialites and literary friends of Horace Walpole (see notes). Sir John Archer rebuilt the house in 1890. In 1968 it was sold, along with its grounds, to the Council, and demolished to further enhance the famous view from Richmond Hill.

Top: Hornby and Clarke built a model dairy at the Petersham Farm in River Lane in the 1870s. The lease was taken over by Express Dairies in 1935, but they continued to trade under the same name. Features of the farm were the spotlessly clean white-tiled byres, and the farm dairy, also tiled, with its cooling and bottling plant. In 1957 Express Dairies took over local milk distribution from Lou Secrett at Ham Manor Farm (see page 20). The Petersham herd of dairy cows then supplied milk to the district until the 1980s. The lease for the farm passed into private hands in 1982, when milk production ceased and a grazier maintained a beef herd on the meadows

An early 1900s photo of the river towards Richmond *(reproduced by kind permission of Sir David Williams)* and the same view today

Right: The Great River Race, an annual event with the Star and Garter Home in the background, September 2002
Photo by David Yates

Above: An engraving by T A Prior from a
painting by T Allom of a river pageant in honour
of Queen Victoria's visit to the Duke of
Buccleuch in June 1842
*Reproduction by kind permission of the Local
Studies Library, Richmond*

Right: A portrait of Mary and Agnes Berry taken
from the *Journals and Correspondence of Mary
Berry* (see notes). While staying in Paris in July
1836, Mary writes in her journal: *'It is now that I
figure Petersham and our quiet garden there is
everything on earth that I most covet and from
which I no longer desire to wander. There in the
immediate neighbourhood of a friend* (Lady
Caroline Lucy Scott of Douglas House), *more my
child than any other ever can be – there I feel that
I can patiently wait for the last stroke which is to
send me to the neighbouring country church-yard*
(at St Peter's church), *where I have long intended
to have my bones deposited.'*

On the hillside in Richmond, which was once celebrated for the song of
nightingales, stands the Petersham Hotel. The hotel was designed by John
Giles and built in the French Gothic style in 1865. It was originally called
'Richmond Hill', then became 'Mansion', then the Star and Garter. It was
renamed under new ownership in 1978 and extensively renovated in 1987.

The site of the Royal Star and Garter Home for Disabled Sailors, Soldiers and
Airmen was originally occupied by an inn, built in 1738 on a corner of
Petersham Common leased from the Dysarts. The inn was enlarged in the
1770s and it was at this time that Captain George Vancouver (see page 92),
on entering the dining room and seeing the view of the Thames from the
window, was reported to have said: *'In all my travels, I have never clapt eyes
on a more beautiful spot than this! Here would I live and here would I die!'*

In the early 1800s, the owner, James Brewer, having further enlarged the
building to attract the fashionable society from London, over-extended
himself and ended his days in the debtors' prison. The hotel was closed for a
time before Christopher Crean, a former cook to the Duke of York, brother of
George IV, took it on and under his management it became a very expensive
and exclusive establishment. In 1812 Joseph Ellis, father of John Whittaker
Ellis (see page 97), took on the lease and it was under his ownership that the
hotel became famous, and a favourite haunt of rich Londoners from the
social world. It was frequented by Charles Dickens (see page 110) who gave
regular dinners there.

In 1864, the hotel was sold and new additions were made at each end of the
building; designed by Edward Middleton Barry, in the style of a French
renaissance château. Extra accommodation and a new banqueting hall were
provided. In February 1870, disaster struck – a great fire destroyed the old
building but left the Barry extensions, including the banqueting hall, little
damaged. In 1874 a new and lavish Italian Romanesque structure was built to
replace the old hotel, between Barry's later additions. C J Phipps, who later
became a famous theatre designer, was the architect.

The rebuilt hotel never recovered its reputation and its popularity declined. It was closed in 1907 and was used in the First World War as temporary accommodation for soldiers and then as a hospital for disabled ex-servicemen. After the war, funds were raised to rebuild the home and the old hotel buildings were replaced by the present Star and Garter Home. Designed by the architect Sir Edwin Cooper RA, the new building was opened by King George V and Queen Mary in 1924. It has become fondly known as the 'Home on the Hill' but having served for over 80 years the large home is no longer considered appropriate for the current and future needs of its residents and new more modern accommodation is being found. At the time of writing (2009), the future of the building is uncertain.

Petersham Common is the tract of land covering just over 17 acres on the steep hill in front of the Star and Garter Home. Most of the 18th and 19th century paintings of 'the View from Richmond Hill' were painted from the upper part of this Common. Now densely wooded, it would have been grazed well into the 19th century, when it was part of the Dysart estate. The Common was one of the areas of land that were transferred to Richmond Corporation by the Dysarts in accordance with the 1902 Richmond, Petersham and Ham Open Spaces Act. It is managed now by the Petersham Common Conservators, residents of Petersham who are elected at the Annual Vestry meeting. There used to be almshouses on the Common, alongside the Petersham Road towards Richmond, which were demolished in 1953.

The present Petersham Road along the lower part of Petersham Common was constructed in 1773 to replace the ancient road that used to run at the extreme foot of the slope, now a track road to the new Petersham Farm buildings and beyond to the Meadows. This lower road was liable to flooding and often impassable.

One of the finest of the Petersham mansions was Petersham Lodge, which stood in Richmond Park, just inside the Petersham Gate, opposite the Dysart Arms. It was originally the home of the Lords of the Manors of Ham and Petersham, the Cole family.

George Cole had been granted a lease of the manors of Ham and Petersham by the Crown. We know little more than the fact that George was a member of the Middle Temple and was married at St Peter's Church in 1585. Both George and his wife Frances were interred in a vault in the church of St Peter's and are commemorated by an imposing monument with their recumbent effigies on the north side of the chancel. They had thirteen children, seven of whom predeceased their father. In 1637 Gregory Cole, George Cole's eldest surviving son, and his wife Anne sold all the Cole property for inclusion in Charles I's New Park (now known as Richmond Park), and left Petersham. Their leasehold rights in the manors of Ham and Petersham were assigned to William Murray, later 1st Earl of Dysart.

Ludowick Carlile, a friend of Murray, was assigned the Petersham manor house henceforward known as Petersham Lodge. For an annual salary of £50 Carlile had been appointed by Charles I to the office of Keeper of the lodge and the walk (a tract of ground on which the deer were kept) at Petersham. As well as a poet and dramatist, Ludowick was 'Gentleman of the Bows' to King Charles I and a 'Groom of the Privy Chamber' to Queen Henrietta Maria. His wife Joan, also known as Anne, was a distinguished portrait painter. Ludowick's first play *The Deserving Favourite*, a tragi-comedy, was dedicated to William Murray.

Just before the Civil War Thomas Knyvett recorded visits to Petersham Lodge. Knyvett, who came from Norfolk was taken prisoner by the Parliamentary forces and charged with having taken part in the abortive uprising at Lowestoft at the beginning of the war in 1643. He was imprisoned for a time in Windsor Castle and then released with restrictions on his movements. His estates were sequestered and he had to stay near London to answer the charges made against him and to attempt to free his estates. Earlier he had stayed at the home of his royalist friends at Petersham Lodge and in 1642 wrote to his wife '*Mr Carlile and his wife ar very willing to soiurne us at ther country house, wch I take extreame kindly from them. They will furnish with all necessaryes but Linning* (linen)'. . . . And in 1644, '*This is a sweet place, & the nightingales doe singe most meleodiously . . . .*'

After the execution of Charles I in 1649, Parliament presented New Park to the City of London '*as an Ornament to the City and a Mark of Favour from the Parliament unto the said City*'. Carlile, together with his son James, continued as keepers throughout the Commonwealth, despite the fact that they were staunch royalists, and Petersham Lodge offered lodgings to many of their cavalier friends.

At the time of the Restoration in 1660 the Park was returned to Charles II, and he appointed his old friend Sir Lionel Tollemache and his wife the Countess of Dysart as Park Rangers. The positions of Park Rangers and Keepers were sinecures, Crown appointments that offered rewards and status for the incumbents with only nominal duties and responsibilities. Colonel Thomas Panton of Petersham House took the place of Carlile as Keeper at Petersham Lodge in 1663. After Sir Lionel's death in 1669 the position of Ranger was transferred to the Countess's second husband, the Duke of Lauderdale.

In 1683 Laurence Hyde (1642–1711), 1st Earl of Rochester, the younger son of Edward Hyde 1st Earl of Clarendon, was made Ranger of the Park and granted a personal lease of Petersham Lodge together with 50 acres of parkland. Lord Rochester was uncle to both Queen Mary and Queen Anne, and Lord High Treasurer of England. An influential politician, he was a courtier during the reigns of Charles II, James II, and William and Mary. He was a stout Anglican and high Tory, was well educated in the literary and visual arts, and is credited with the publication of his father's *History of the Rebellion*.

Above: A 1710 engraving, entitled *New Park in Surry, Seat of the Rt Honble the Earle of Rochester* by Johannes Kip from a drawing by Leonard Knyff for *Britannia Illustrata*. The house stood on flat ground to the west and the gardens, which stretched 140 feet above the house to the south and east, were laid out with formal parterres, spectacular terraces and orchards, cut into the hillside. The formal landscape then opened out into a wilderness of woodland with many avenues, all diversified by rills and fountains, up to King Henry VIII's Mound

Opposite: The 1624 Cole monument on the north wall of the chancel of St Peter's church. The recumbent effigies of George Cole and his wife Frances lie along with their grandson who died just before his grandfather at the age of 4

It was the 1st Earl of Rochester who in 1693, when he was out of office, replaced the old Petersham Lodge with a classical and fine, but sadly short-lived, mansion for his country seat. The name was changed from Petersham Lodge to New Park. The building was probably designed by Robert Hooke and built under the supervision of the architect Matthew Banckes, who was Master Carpenter to the Office of Works from 1683 to 1706. Formal gardens and spectacular terraces were laid out, the work of Henry Wise, Banckes' son-in-law and Queen Anne's royal gardener, and George London.

Samuel Molyneux visited New Park in 1712–1713 and described it thus in his letter book: '. . . . *if Hampton Court did not fill my Expectation the Gardens here I assure you did pay the Pains of my Journey and gave me perfect Satisfaction. I think I have never yet seen any piece of Gardening that has so much as this the true taste of Beauty . . . . The Partere behind the house and the Hornbeam walks beyond it are well enough but a very high hill to the left of the Gardens part of which is beautifully and wildly dispos'd into Slopes, the rest and upper part cover'd with a fine wood so interspers'd with Vistas & little innumerable private dark walks thro' every part of it lin'd on both sides with low hedges with the unconfin'd Prospects you meet every now and then of the*

Garden below the Country and the River beyond you is what in my opinion makes the Particular & distinguish'd preferable beauty of this place – beyond any thing that I have ever yet seen. I should not forget to tell you that in every walk you meet here and there a little opening in the wood with Seats, a Statue, a grass plott, a Basin of water or the like, for you must know that here is a Fountain playing on the side of the hill (the Spring being at the Top) which is much higher, the Basin of which lyes higher than the house Roof as well as I remember they shew'd us here a huge Cedar of Libanus . . . .'

New Park was inherited by Henry Hyde (1672–1753), 2nd Earl of Rochester and 4th Earl of Clarendon, when his father died suddenly in 1711. Henry also succeeded his father as Park Ranger, holding the position until 1727. He married the beautiful Jane Leveson-Gower (1672–1725), who was much admired by poets of the day including Matthew Prior and Jonathan Swift. *'You find a fine house at the bottom of the Hill, built by the late Earl of Rochester, Uncle to the late Queen, whose Gardens ascending the Hill in an artful confus'd manner, are very curious and wonderful.'* John Macky, *A Journey through England, in familiar letters from a Gentleman here to his friend Abroad 1722–3.*

Henry and Jane Hyde had eight children, including Kitty who later became the Duchess of Queensberry, of Douglas House, (see page 119) and Lady Jane who married the Earl of Essex at St Peter's Church in 1718. According to the Weekly Journal or British Gazetteer: *'near two hundred Persons of Quality were invited to the Celebrating of their Nuptials.'*

In October 1721 Jane Hyde and her family were fortunate to survive the catastrophic destruction of most of New Park in a fire which consumed not only valuable furniture and pictures but also the magnificent library of Henry Hyde's grandfather, the 1st Earl of Clarendon.

In late 1721 or early 1720 Daniel Defoe (see notes) wrote:
'But keeping the river now on my left, as I did before on my right-hand, drawing near to London, we came to Hame and Peterson, little villages; the first, famous for a most pleasant pallace of the late Duke of Lauderdale, close by the river; a house King Charles II used to be frequently at, and be exceedingly pleased with; the avenues of this fine house to the land side, come up to the end of the village of Peterson, where the wall of New

Park comes also close to the town, on the other side; in an angle of which stood a most delicious house, built by the late Earl of Rochester, Lord High Treasurer in King James II's reign, as also in part of Queen Ann's reign, which place he discharged so well, that we never heard of any misapplications, so much as suggested, much less inquired after. I am oblig'd to say only, that this house stood here; for even while this is writing the place seems to be but smoking with the ruins of a most unhappy disaster; the whole house being a few months ago burnt down to the ground with a fire, so sudden, and so furious, that the family who were all at home, had scarce time to save their lives.

'Nor was the house, tho' so exquisitely finished, so beautiful within and without, the greatest loss sustained; the rich furniture, the curious collection of paintings; and above all, the most curious collection of books, being the library of the first Earl of Clarendon, Lord Chancellor of England, and author of that most

The first visual records we can find of Lord Burlington's building are two prints of c.1752 by Augustin Heckel, a native of Augsburg, Germany. This one is the view of the Earl of Harrington's House (as it was then known) from the garden, now part of Richmond Park. St Peter's church spire (before it was replaced with the cupola) can be seen on the far left, on the other side of the Petersham Road. Note also the slope of the hill on the right, where the formally laid out gardens were once situated

Overleaf is a view of the same house from the front
Both prints reproduced by kind permission of Martin Rice-Edwards

excellent History of the Rebellion, of which the world knows so much; I say, this library, as I am assur'd, was here wholly consumed; a loss irreparable, and not to be sufficiently regretted by all lovers of learning, having among other valuable things, several manuscripts relating to those times, and to things transacted by himself, and by the king his master, both at home and abroad; and of other antient things, collected by that noble and learned author in foreign countries; which both for their rarity, antiquity, and authority, were of an inestimable value.'

Ten years later William Stanhope (1683–1756), 1st Earl of Harrington, diplomat and statesman, bought the lease of the estate and in about 1733 he commissioned the 'architect Earl' Richard Boyle, 3rd Earl of Burlington, to design a new building on the site. The architect Earl was described by Horace Walpole as *'the Apollo of the Arts'*, famous for his designs for Chiswick House and Tottenham Park, Wiltshire. Once more the house became known as Petersham Lodge. It was a long low building, much less imposing than New Park. In a further development in 1740, covered colonnades and octagonal pavilions were added, designed by the architect Edward Shepherd. The 1746 John Rocque map shows that much of the landscape had once more reverted to parkland, with no trace of the old formal gardens.

The finest work of the Scottish poet and Richmond resident James Thomson (1700–48) was his cycle of poems *The Seasons*, written over the years 1726–30. In *Summer* (see notes), published in 1727, he wrote:
'*. . . . To where the silver Thames first rural grows.*
There let the feasted eye unwearied stray;
Luxurious, there, rove thro' the pendant woods
That nodding hang o'er Harrington's retreat;
And, stooping thence to Ham's embowering walks,
Beneath whose shades in spotless peace retir'd
With Her, the pleasing partner of his heart,
The worthy Queensb'ry yet laments his Gay;
And polish'd Cornbury woos the willing Muse.
Slow let us trace the matchless Vale of Thames . . . .'

In 1756 William 2nd Earl of Harrington (1719–79) inherited the house, which at this time was usually known as 'Lord Harrington's'. On William's death in 1779 the 3rd Earl, General Charles Stanhope (1753–1829), previously known as Lord Petersham, sold the Lodge and grounds to the politician and art connoisseur Thomas Pitt (1737–93), later Lord Camelford. Repairs and alterations to the Lodge were made for him by Sir John Soane in 1781. In 1791 Pitt sold the Lodge to the Duke of Clarence, later King William IV, who renamed the house Clarence Lodge. Previously, William had leased Ivy Hall (see page 43) for a few months in 1789 as a retreat from his London home at St James's Palace.

At the time of his move to Petersham Lodge, Dora Jordan (née Dorothy Bland) became the Duke's mistress, and was his consort for some twenty years, bearing him ten children. Their eldest son, the Earl of Munster, was born here. Mrs Jordan came from an Irish acting family and began to make her mark on the London stage from 1785, appearing regularly at both the Richmond Theatre and at Drury Lane. Their scandalous attachment was much satirised at the time by cartoonists, particularly Gillray and Cruickshank. In 1797 William's father King George III presented him with the royal estate at Bushy House near Hampton Court Palace.

Two years earlier, Sir William Manners, later Lord Huntingtower, the eldest son of Louisa, 7th Countess of Dysart, bought the Lodge from the Duke. He and his family adopted the name Tollemache, his mother's maiden name, in 1821. He was the father of Algernon and Frederick Tollemache (see page 40), who were both born here. Their elder brother Lionel Tollemache, 8th Earl of Dysart, asked them to manage the Buckminster estates for him. They both moved to Ham House and as well as running the estate acted, singly or together, as Lords of the Manor. Frederick was the more active, and was also one of the founder members of the Ham Local Board which took over the responsibilities of the Ham Vestry in 1862.

In 1835 the house, now in some decay having not been regularly occupied for some twenty years, together with 59 acres of land, was sold by the executors of Lord Huntingtower to the Commissioners of Woods and Forests, by whom it was entirely destroyed and the grounds were once again incorporated with Richmond Park. All that remains today of the formal gardens of New Park are

Above: The Hon Frederick James Tollemache (1804–88) younger brother of Lionel, 8th Earl of Dysart. In 1847 he married Isobella Anne, the daughter of Gordon Forbes of Forbes House on Ham Common (see page 40). This marriage only lasted 3 years as she died in 1850. Their only daugter Ada Maria married Charles Hanbury-Tracy, 4th Baron Sudeley (see pages 52-3). Frederick, his younger brother Algernon and for a time Lord Sudeley were trustees of the Dysart estate

Reproduced by kind permission of Merlin, 7th Lord Sudeley

The 18th century cedar trees in Richmond Park today

Above: The view of St Paul's cathedral, ten miles away in the city of London, and James Batten looking at the view through the telescope on King Henry's Mound

some of the spectacular 18th century cedars and the prehistoric mound near Pembroke Lodge depicted in Knyff and Kip's engraving of 1710 (see page 79).

King Henry's Mound presents views that have delighted visitors to Richmond Park for many years. To the west a panoramic view can be seen over Petersham and Ham House to Windsor Castle. To the east is the unique 'keyhole' Vista of St Paul's Cathedral, some ten miles away in the City and towards which an avenue had been planted within the Park in 1710 to commemorate the completion of St. Paul's that year. In 1976 James Batten, then a committee member of the Ham and Petersham Association, began alerting various authorities to the fact that high-rise development on that axis in Central London would obscure, or cut into, the famous Vista. Through persistent efforts over the years he has battled to save that Vista. In 1992, thanks mainly to him, the Government declared the Vista 'protected'.

However, the viewing corridor is under constant pressure from ill-advised development. In 2002 the then Mayor of London, Ken Livingstone, produced his Mayor's London Plan, a blueprint for the capital's growth which effectively removed the protection, and under new planning rules in 2005 the viewing corridor was to be reduced by 50%, from a width of about 150m left to right at the Cathedral. However in 2008 the new Mayor, Boris Johnson, declared that he would safeguard the great Vista by reverting to the original Government protection granted in 1992.

In 2000 the Ham and Petersham Association, whose Chairman at that time was Sylvia Peile, led a campaign to keep the existing gates of Richmond Park open to traffic. A Royal Parks Review by Dame Jennifer Jenkins in 1996 had identified that traffic was the most contentious issue facing the Park. A proposal was put forward to close some of the Park gates to traffic, including the Ham Gate, and to reduce the speed limit to 20 mph. Some 800 protestors marched through the park to voice their disapproval of gate closures. In the event, although the Robin Hood Gate on the A3 was closed to traffic and the speed limit put in place, the fear of Ham and Petersham being cut off did not materialise as the other park gates remained open.

Pembroke Lodge is a notable Georgian mansion which sits on the highest point in the Park and has spectacular views across the Thames valley to Windsor and over Surrey. Originally a molecatcher's cottage it was extended to the house we see today by Elizabeth Herbert, Countess of Pembroke who was principal lady-in-waiting to George III. In 1847 Queen Victoria granted the house to Prime Minister Lord John Russell. In 1854 the Cabinet met at Pembroke Lodge and decided to proceed with the Crimean War against Russia. It was the childhood home of Lord John Russell's grandson, Bertrand Russell (1872–1970), 3rd Earl Russell, philosopher, mathematician, Nobel prize-winner for literature in 1950 and prolific author. After decades of dereliction it has been recently restored by the Hearsum family to provide a well-run restaurant and wedding venue.

Lord John Russell was one of the authors of the 1832 Reform Bill which doubled the British electorate. Although he was a member of the Church of England, Russell was a firm believer in civil and religious liberty and keen to promote non-denominational schools for children from poorer homes. In 1852 he and his wife Fanny put his ideas into practice by establishing Petersham British School, the first Russell Primary School. The school started with 12 boys and 12 girls on a small plot of land in Richmond Park, at the bottom of the Star and Garter Hill, made available under a Royal Warrant for the education of the poor.

In 1891, the Russells' interest in the school was transferred to the Trustees of the British and Foreign School Society which was originally formed for the advancement of education for the poor. It continued as the village school until November 1943 when it was damaged beyond repair by enemy bombs in the Second World War. It was replaced in 1954 by the Orchard Junior School on the Petersham Road together with the adjoining Petersham Russell Infants' School; these have since been combined as the Russell School.

Above: Lord John Russell in 1865
Reproduced by kind permission of Daniel Hearsum

The old school tuckshop that was once on the other side of the Petersham Road from the Russell School, next door to Fountain Cottage

Right: A guide plan of Richmond Park dated 1876. If this map appears confusing, note that it was drawn with south-east at the top

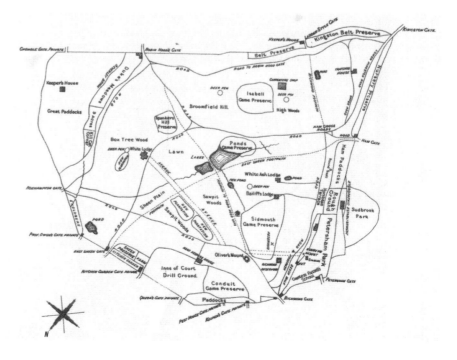

Above, top: Early 1900s photos of the old Russell School buildings from the west, just opposite the Dysart Arms. They were destroyed by a Second World War incendiary bomb

Above, middle left: A bus coming down into Petersham Village opposite the old Russell school. Petersham Vale is on the left. Note the amusing signpost!
Reproduced by kind permission of Sir David Williams

Above, middle right: A 1930 photo by Roy Emerson, which was on sale at the old Petersham Post Office where he worked. It shows the bend in the road at the bottom of the Star and Garter Hill, looking west to the start of Petersham village. The old Russell School buildings can be seen behind the park wall on the left. The gates to the Old Petersham Lodge can be seen on the extreme left of the picture and, a little way down the wall, the archway over the water fountain fed from a spring, from which Fountain Cottage took its name. Until the early 1900s a donkey and cart would be driven here daily from Ham House to fill up with the precious spring water

A 1900s photo of Petersham village from the slope of the hill in Richmond Park *(reproduced by kind permission of Sir David Williams)*, and the same view today

The old inn on the site of the present Dysart Arms, known as the Plough and Harrow, with its oak beams, leaded windows and charming window boxes, probably dated from around the second half of the 17th century and was originally a farmhouse. It is reported that the Countess of Dysart paid for the name to be changed in the 1830s, though this is not substantiated. The building was pulled down in 1902 and replaced by the Arts and Crafts – inspired inn that we see today.

Above: Julian Barrow painted this view of Parkgate in the late 1970's. Although some licence has been taken with the perspective, it shows how Petersham would have looked, little changed from the mid 1800s

Above left: The front porch of Parkgate today. The rounded bays and the columned front porch were added in the early 19th century

Opposite: A c.1852 photograph of the Dysart Arms by George Hilditch
Reproduced by kind permission of the Local Studies Library, Richmond

The new building for the Dysart Arms was designed by the architect John Shewell Corder, from East Anglia. He was well regarded for his medieval timbered buildings in Norfolk and Suffolk and for his sensitive and painstaking restoration of such buildings as the famous Guild Hall in Lavenham and for the inspiration he drew from these buildings and their hand craftsmanship for his commissions, in tune with the Arts and Crafts ethos of the period. His design of the Dysart Arms used materials of very high quality, such as the oak and carvings that grace it. The photographs (opposite) taken in 2014 show how little change there has been to the main facade.

Opposite, left: An interesting pre Second World War aerial photo of Petersham showing Douglas House on the right. Petersham Lodge in River Lane, Rutland Lodge, Petersham House and Reston Lodge can be seen clearly on the left and All Saints church is in the background
Reproduced by kind permission of Bill Crossley

The main front of Parkgate was added to an earlier cottage in the late 18th century. It was built by the licensee Allan Blizzard of the Plough and Harrow (now the Dysart Arms) next door. Blizzard had also aquired Church House and sold it to the Marquess of Bute in 1805 (see Bute House, page 96). The Ashford family (see Elm Lodge, page 110) lived at Parkgate for a time before moving to Sussex.

Church House may well have been the site of the imposing house with four chimneys which is depicted in the van Diest painting (see page 68). The hearth tax of 1664 shows that a Mr John Goodyer was assessed for five hearths and this may account for the four chimneys. In about 1800 some of the land was made over to enlarge St Peter's churchyard and another part became the site of Parkgate.

In the mid 19th century Church House was the home of Paul Coutts Stuart, the only son of the Coutts Stuarts of Bute House (see page 96). This is the 'white house' mentioned in the sale particulars as being linked to Bute House by a subterraneous passage. The passage existed until about 1970 when it was bricked up by the council to prevent subsidence of the Petersham Road. Church House had come into the ownership of the Bute family in 1805 and was rebuilt in 1838, having fallen into a dilapidated state.

Captain Paul Amadeus Francis Coutts Stuart suffered from a mild form of mental illness and was a recluse; he died at the age of 63 in 1889 and is buried at St Peter's Church. As he had no close relatives, Church House was left to his mother's younger brother Prince Louis-Lucien, who was Napoleon's nephew. Captain Stuart never knew his uncle who was a French anglophile linguist, particularly noted for his scholarly work with regard to the Basque language. It was the Prince who erected the tombstone for his nephew at St Peter's Church.

St Peter's Church, with its small red-brick steeple surmounted by a cupola, stands at the south-east corner of the Petersham Meadows, tucked away from the busy Petersham Road. It is mentioned in the Domesday Book of 1086, and it is quite likely that there was already a church here in Saxon times. The oldest part that can be seen today is the blocked lancet window in the north wall of the chancel which dates back to the Norman church built here in the 13th century. The rebuilding of the church in 1505 provided much of its present fabric, extending west to and including the lower part of the tower. Further enlargements came in the next century when two small transepts and a small gallery on the north side were built, producing a unique interior where most of the pews do not face the altar. The notable compartment box pews are some of the last remaining in England and reflect the high social standing of some of the congregation who paid for the privilege of their place in the church. By 1720 the present cupola had replaced the spire and in 1790 the west porch and vestry were built. The impressive pulpit with its original candle holders, raised high above the pews, was built in 1796 by John Long, a local carpenter.

In 1840 the south transept was considerably enlarged; new galleries built, and the church today is little changed since that time. There are a number of interesting internal monuments, particularly the lavish Elizabethan memorial to the Lord of the Manor, George Cole (see page 78), his wife, and his grandson and namesake; also a tablet in memory of Sir Thomas Jenner of Montrose House (see page 100). There are vaults under almost the entire floor space of the church. Within the chancel were buried many of the Dysart family, including Elizabeth, Duchess of Lauderdale, who died in 1698. The monuments, together with those in St Peter's exceptionally large and extended churchyard, are a testament to Petersham's long history as a country retreat for the aristocracy, many of whom were buried here. Among other well-known names to be found in the churchyard are those of Captain George Vancouver (see page 92); the great-grandchildren of William Penn, the founder of Pennsylvania; Agnes and Mary Berry, the friends of Horace Walpole (see Devonshire Lodge, page 74); and the publisher Jonathan Cape. In fact, as James Thorne wrote in his *Handbook to the Environs of London* in 1876, '*The ch-yard contains the remains of many persons eminent in place or merit*'. More details are given in Charles D Warren's comprehensive history of the church.

Colonel Thomas Panton (see notes) built the first Petersham House between 1663 and 1677 at the time he became Keeper of the Park. Originally, it was a two-storey house surmounted by a cupola; the third storey was probably added in the early 19th century, at the same time as the magnificent semi-circular and domed Ionic porch.

Prominent owners of Petersham House (see notes) include Sir Henry Furnese, a notable city merchant and politician and his son Sir Robert, the Halhed family and also Lucy, Dowager Duchess of Rutland, who died in 1751.

Described by Arthur T Bolton in *Country Life* (1918) as *'a singularly interesting house'*, Petersham House has an interior staircase from the Wren period as well as classical mythological wall paintings of about 1710 by the French decorative painter Louis Laguerre. The mantelpieces are a notable feature of the house, three of them dating from the 1770s. The garden is sometimes open to the public under the National Gardens Scheme. It has a beautiful 150 ft long herbaceous border and particularly fine wrought-iron gates at the bottom. The kitchen garden supplies some of its produce to the neighbouring Petersham Nursery for use in its café and restaurant.

Above: Petersham House

Below: Rutland Lodge from the front, and right: from a lithograph by Thomas R Way, 1900 *(reproduced by kind permission of the Local Studies Library, Richmond)*

Opposite, above: An early 1900s photo of St Peter's church and Petersham House from what was then known as the Walnut Tree field *(reproduced by kind permission of Sir David Williams)* and the same view from a lithograph by Thomas R Way, 1900 *(reproduced by kind permission of the Local Studies Library, Richmond)*

Left: The Petersham Nursery and the long border to the rear of Petersham House in the summer

Rutland Lodge was built in about 1720 on the site of an older two-storey, L-shaped building, which is thought to have been the final home of Sir Thomas Jenner (see Montrose House, page 100). The Lodge was inherited by his youngest daughter, Margaret, and it was she who erected the monument to her father on the south wall of the chancel at St Peter's Church. She married Sir John Darnall, and they, most likely, built the fine Georgian house that we see today. The monogram on its wrought-iron gate is probably that of the Darnall family.

On the death of Dame Margaret, their daughter Mary inherited the house; she also owned Petersham Lodge on River Lane (see page 93). She married Robert Ord, Chief Baron of the Exchequer of Scotland and head of the judiciary, and on her death Rutland Lodge passed into the ownership of their son John Ord, also a politician, who in 1790 sold the house to the 5th Earl of Dysart.

The house was included in the auction of the Dysarts' Ham and Petersham estate in 1949. Sadly the interior was entirely destroyed by fire in 1967. Now it is only possible to see in photographs the extent of the decorative interior, including a handsome and spacious staircase which ascended to the principal room on the first floor and a magnificent fireplace. Demolition was considered after the fire but fortunately the building was saved by local residents who formed the Petersham Society and secured a temporary preservation order on the building which the Greater London Council then made permanent. It was converted into flats, a new residential wing was added to the west and two new small houses were built in the grounds at the rear, in Rutland Drive.

It is a mystery why the house was called 'Rutland' as there is no evidence that Dukes and Duchesses of Rutland ever lived there, though their name is associated with both Montrose House and Petersham House.

The history of River Lane, which leads from the Petersham Road down to the river, can be traced back to 1617. Both the Manor House and Petersham Cottage next door at 147 Petersham Road are shown on the Rocque map of 1746, but not the Manor Farm House. The 'Manor House', which in its present form probably dates from the early 18th century, does not appear to have ever been the manor house of Petersham. The extensive farm buildings on the south side of the Farm House were demolished in the early years of the present century. Two innovative houses, the Drum House and Courtyards, were designed by Leonard Manasseh and built off the lane in 1964–7. In 2004 Terry Farrell and Partners were chosen to design a further development in the grounds of Courtyards, known as the Three Houses. These three individual family homes form part of a contemporary high-quality architectural grouping whilst remaining totally private. The scheme won the National Housebuilders Award in that year.

Glen Cottage in River Lane is where Captain George Vancouver (1758-98), the explorer and surveyor, is said to have written his famous *Voyage of Discovery to the North Pacific and around the World*. He spent the last two years of his short life here. He surveyed the west coast of North America, including what became British Columbia. He also sailed with Captain Cook to Antarctica and was with him on his last fatal voyage to the Pacific. An annual service of commemoration is held each May at his simple tombstone in the churchyard of St Peter's.

Glen Cottage was sold by the Dysarts in the 1949 Ham and Petersham estate auction. It became the home of Geoffry Powell who died here in 1999. He was a partner of Chamberlin, Powell & Bon, the architects chosen by the City Corporation in the mid-1950s to design the Barbican Centre, a commission that dominated Powell's career for nearly three decades.

The first building on the site of Petersham Lodge in River Lane can be traced back to 1617. Mary, wife of Robert Ord and daughter of Sir John Darnall (see Rutland Lodge), bought a house here in 1744. Seven years later John Ord, Mary's son, inherited it from her, and it was then sold to Sir Henry Bellenden, Gentleman Usher of the Black Rod. Bellenden died in 1761, leaving the house to his nephew Lord Frederick Campbell, son of the 4th Duke of Argyll. There were then various owners until 1850 when the house had become dilapidated. Richard Powney, an artillery colonel in the service of the East India Company and later a General, obtained a licence at the Manor Court to demolish the premises, provided that at least the full value was spent on betterment. The new Georgian style building that we see today was called Petersham Lodge, taking on the same name as the original Petersham Lodge in Richmond Park (see page 82) some 15 years after it was pulled down.

In 1902 it was purchased by Sir Max Waechter (1837–1924) to save it from the threat of development and to help preserve the view from Richmond Hill. Sir Max, who was German by birth and lived on Richmond Hill Terrace, was a businessman, philanthropist, art collector, and High Sheriff of Surrey who in later life lobbied heads of state with his scheme for a Federation of the Peoples of Europe. By presenting both Petersham Ait (also known as Glover's Island) and Petersham Lodge to Richmond, he made an important contribution to the preservation of the open view from Richmond Hill.

Richmond Council accepted his gift of the freehold of Petersham Lodge with
restricted covenants as to building, and granted a 99-year lease to the then
Princess of Wales, later Queen Mary, who *'wanted to provide a place where
poor governesses might spend their holidays amid happy surroundings free of
expense to themselves'*. The home, which was open for two months at Easter,
three months during the summer and one month at Christmas, was
maintained by endowment and by voluntary contributions, and in the year
1925 Petersham Lodge received visits from as many as 61 governesses from
around the country.

But by 1945 the concept of genteel and impoverished governesses was
outdated, and the charity administering the home then surrendered its lease
to Richmond Council. In putting the lease on the market, the Council decided
to reduce the grounds from some six acres to three. Sadly, the summerhouse
overlooking the river at the end of the Petersham Lodge garden, built in the
latter part of the 18th century, was demolished.

This part of the Petersham Lodge garden became known as Petersham Lodge
Woods. Recently designated as a Nature Reserve, it has suffered from lack of
funding and neglect and some of the fine collection of mature trees are in a
sorry state. The central avenue of horse chestnuts and the fine colossal
Oriental Plane that survive are particularly noteworthy.

In the early 18th century Bute House and its 10-acre estate, the site of the present-day Cedar Heights and Bute Avenue, was the property of the Duke of Argyll, who lived at Sudbrook Park. The estate came into the ownership of the Bute family in 1785. James Stuart Mackenzie (1719–1800) was the younger brother of the 3rd Earl of Bute who was George III's first minister. He married his first cousin, Lady Elizabeth Campbell, the third daughter of the Duke of Argyll (see Sudbrook Park, page 112). Stuart added the surname Mackenzie when he inherited extensive estates in Scotland from his great-grandfather. In 1800 he left the Bute House estate to his nephew John Stuart, Marquess of Bute (1744–1814).

Little is known about Bute House prior to 1800. There may have been originally two houses which were knocked into one. But the Marquess made major alterations to what became a very large house and in 1805 the architect Robert Mylne, who built The Wick on Richmond Hill, designed a classical façade for him. The Marquess of Bute's second wife Frances, a daughter of the banker Thomas Coutts, inherited the property on the Marquess's death in 1814, and from her it passed in 1832 to their only son, Lord Dudley Coutts Stuart who also owned at this time the Manor House in Ham. As MP for Arundel, and later for Marylebone, Coutts Stuart was one of the foremost supporters of the First Reform Bill. He was also a supporter of Liberal causes abroad, particularly the plight of Polish refugees. In 1824 he married Princess Christine Alexandrine Egypta, daughter of Prince Lucien Bonaparte, 1st Prince of Canino, the younger brother of Napoleon. They did not live at Bute House but rented it out, and it seems that the estate was put on the market in 1833. *The Times* on 21 May of that year recorded the following sale announcement, the text of which is given in full as it beats any modern day estate agent's description!

At Petersham by Mr George Robins at the Auction Mart on Tuesday next, June 18 at 12. An elegant MANSION, many years the favourite retreat of the Dowager Marchioness of Bute, at Petersham with corresponding offices of every description. This singularly desirable abode, which is copyhold of inheritance, hath for many a long year been distinguished for its superior accommodation; it probably rests its principal claim upon the comfort that will be found to preside within. During the last few years the Marchioness has expended upwards of £2,000 in substantial repairs. The back part is the most commanding, and without pretending to strict architectural form, it presents a noble elevation, commanding, in every direction, a perfect view of the delightful grounds the disposition of which is in such excellent taste that the palm of superiority has long been conceded to it. There are two kitchen gardens (nearly 3 acres), with a conservatory well placed. Within the chateau will be found all the accommodation a distinguished family can in reason desire. It would occupy too much space to give in detail its never-ending accommodation. It may suffice to state the grand suite of spacious rooms are in communication with the picture gallery, and thence to the extensive pleasure grounds, its verdant lawn, and shrubbery walks. The secondary apartments are in strict keeping with the whole, and as regards the offices enclosed in the court yard they will be found to include everything that the most fastidious can desire. A subterraneous passage leads to the white house opposite, (Church House, see page 87) and was frequently very useful as an auxiliary, when the great house was full of company. This might at a small expense be rendered a very snug little cottage villa. The domain, including the park meadows, exceeds 10 acres of land and it may be affirmed very safely that there is nothing in the delightful vicinity comparable with the one under consideration. It can be viewed only with tickets and particulars one month antecedently to the sale, at the Mansion, at the Castle, Richmond etc.

By 1871 Bute House had become an 'Academy for the sons of Gentlemen' run by the Revd Charles Godby, with 80 boarding pupils. The school continued throughout the 1880s. Edward N. Radford, a Crimean War veteran, preacher, and butler at Bute House was one of the defendants along with William Harry Harland at the trial over the defence of Ham Common in 1891 (see page 33).

The Bute estate was acquired by Sir John Whittaker Ellis in 1894. He was born in 1829 at the old Star and Garter Hotel of which his father was proprietor, and was Lord Mayor of London in 1881, a MP from 1884 to 1892, and the first Mayor of Richmond in 1890/1. Controversially, he demolished Bute House, intending to build a substantial number of houses on the estate. This plan was not carried through at the time, and in an apparent change of heart he was later to play a prominent part in the campaign against similar developments that eventually led to the 1902 Act protecting the view from Richmond Hill. There were many who wished that the estate be incorporated into the Park to preserve the fine views. A description in *The Times* deploring the eventual demolition of the house in 1895: *'Bute House stood at the entrance to Petersham village. Screened from the road by a high wall, it looked at the back upon an old-fashioned lawn, shaded by a fine cedar. Beyond the lawn stretched an orchard, surrounded by a shrubbery walk and flanked on the right by an extensive walled garden'.*

By the end of the 19th century a new church for Petersham had been under consideration for some time. St Peter's Church was not easy to enlarge and was considered insufficient for the needs of a growing population. When Samuel Walker of Petersham House died in 1898, his daughter Rachel Lætetia Warde became the beneficiary of his large estate. She stepped in to buy the grounds of the Bute House estate to save it (albeit temporarily) from housing development.

Mrs Warde built All Saints Church and its adjoining village hall at the southern end of the estate over the period 1899–1909; both were built in the Romanesque style of red brick and terracotta. The church, a memorial to her parents, has a high tower of 118 ft surmounted by a bronze figure of Christ, and was designed by the architect John Kelly.

The new Village Hall and Institute for Sunday School was opened in 1900. The building was a memorial to her aunt who lived with her brother's family at Petersham House for many years. There is an inscription on the frieze at the front of the building which reads *'AD 1900. Ellen Walker. Thy Kingdom Come. Memorial Church Room'*. Today the hall continues to be used for many local events including the annual Petersham Horticultural Society flower show in July which dates back to 1895. It is also the home of the independent preparatory school known as Sudbrook School.

The church itself was not completed until 1909, by her only son Lionel, as sadly Mrs Warde had died three years before. Lady Sudeley of Reston Lodge opened the building on her behalf. A broad carriageway swept round to All Saints from handsome iron gates on the Petersham Road. This approach was later closed off and houses were built close to the church on Bute Avenue in the 1930s. Further building followed, and by 1970 the houses of Cedar Heights and Ashfield Close were completed.

All Saints Church was not consecrated but was used by the parish congregation until the Second World War when the church (as well as the then Vicarage and Elm Lodge) were requisitioned by Anti-Aircraft Command

and used as an important radar post, training school and research centre. It was twice bombed but rapidly repaired. After the war, although St Peter's remained the Parish Church, All Saints was also sometimes used by the Petersham parish for church services. It was also used by the Greek Orthodox Church, and, because of its excellent acoustics, for commercial recording. It is now a private dwelling and is Grade II listed.

There may have been two Elizabethan cottages on the present Reston Lodge site, but the existing single house was re-built some time in the early 19th century. There is a legend that Prince Rupert of the Rhine, nephew of Charles I, lived in one of the cottages. It is also said that he married Lady Francesca Bard, daughter of Henry Bard, Viscount Bellamont, at St Peter's Church in 1664. Unfortunately the parish registers for that period are incomplete, and if such a marriage contract did exist it was never acknowledged by the Prince.

In the 1770s Reston Lodge was the home of Rebecca, sister of John Bristow of Quidenham, Norfolk and in the 1820s and 30s it was the home of the two unmarried daughters of the 11th Lord Elphinstone. Their youngest sister was married to David Erskine of Cardross who lived next door at Montrose House.

Lady Sudeley moved here from Ormeley Lodge when her husband the 4th Lord Sudeley died in 1922. She took an active part in local affairs, acting as Chairman or President of many local charities and performing various opening ceremonies. In 1939 the Army requisitioned the house and after the war it was the home of the Vines family for over forty years.

Right: Reston Lodge

Opposite: The rich red brick and terracotta All Saints church and Petersham village hall next door

The original Montrose House, which was subsequently enlarged, is said to have been built in the late 17th or early 18th century by Sir Thomas Jenner (1638–1707). He was a notable Catholic judge and staunch Jacobite, appointed Recorder of London in 1683 and knighted at the same time. At the accession of James II he was appointed baron of the exchequer. He was appointed to the Court of Common Pleas in 1688, but when William of Orange's army entered London later in that year he attempted to join James II in the latter's flight into exile, was captured and imprisoned in the Tower of London. Released in 1690, but expelled from the Bench, he resumed private practice as a lawyer, remaining active until 1702. He was regarded as a man of modest talents and accomplishments. Under no illusions as to his abilities, he expressed himself in his diary as *'always doubtful of my own sufficiency to acquit myself in great matters'*. Attempting to excuse his activities before the Commons after the revolution he explained that *'his temptations were great, he had a wife and ten children and but a small estate'*. He died in Petersham in 1707 and was buried in a vault in St Peter's Church. Jenner left Montrose House to his youngest daughter, Margaret Darnall of Rutland Lodge.

In 1814 David Erskine bought the house and lived here until 1835 with his wife, the youngest daughter of 11th Lord Elphinstone. From 1836 until her death in 1847 Caroline Dowager Duchess of Montrose (widow of the 3rd Duke) rented the house, and it was at this time that it acquired her name.

John Henry Master JP and his wife Gertrude Emma lived here from 1883 to 1919. He had been a Collector and Magistrate in India. Gertrude was apparently lame as a result of a fall when someone stepped on her train. She campaigned against cruelty to animals, and was instrumental in forcing the bus company to use an extra horse on the Star and Garter Hill stretch of the Richmond to Kingston bus route. She was also an ardent teetotaller, and in 1889 she founded the Mission Hall and Coffee House called the GEM palace, taken from her initials, to *'promote the spiritual, moral, intellectual and social interests of the poor of Petersham'*. Renamed Trefoil House, 183–185 Petersham Road has since been a Girl Guide Centre, a Women's Institute, a refuge for the school children when the Russell School was bombed in the Second World War and a Church Hall. It has now been divided into private flats.

Montrose House was sold to Philip Carr (chairman of Peak Frean & Co.) in 1919 and to the entertainer Tommy Steele in 1969; the nearby sharp bend in the Petersham Road is still known in the district as Tommy Steele's Corner. His sculpture of Charlie Chaplin was a notable landmark inside the Montrose House gates for many years.

Right: The old Richmond to Kingston horse bus in the early 1900s
Reproduced by kind permission of the Local Studies Library, Richmond

Opposite: Montrose House

That bend in the road has long been a problem. In the 1850s Algernon Tollemache, leader of the 'Trustees of the Roads' committee, persuaded the owners of Montrose House to part with a small portion of their land to reduce the sharpness of the bend. In 1927 there was a proposal by the Ministry of Transport to widen the road to 80ft from the New Inn to Sudbrook Lane, with a new Petersham bypass running from there through the Bute estate to the Dysart Arms. As reported in *The Times* of that year, many houses including Elm Lodge would have had to be demolished. A public meeting was called at the Petersham Village Hall on 28 May 1935. 300 residents attended and petitions against the plans were drawn up. A 'Ham and Petersham Preservation Society' was formed with a committee to organise the petitions. *The Morning Post* of 1st June 1935 publicised the proposals in an article *'Threat to Petersham, the Loveliest Village of the Plain'*. In the event the bypass proposals were shelved. In the 1960s a bypass was again being considered. By this time, the Ham and Petersham Association had been formed and represented residents at a Public Inquiry in 1966. The Inquiry decided that the need for a bypass had been established but the actual route was undecided. Eventually the bypass idea was again dropped, mainly because of the huge financial and environmental implications.

In 1979 the road near the bend was closed for the better part of two years while repairs were made to collapsed drains. Buses had to terminate and run shuttle services, light traffic was diverted through Richmond Park, and all other traffic had a long detour through either Roehampton or Teddington. The Petersham Hole became notorious, and T-shirts proclaiming 'I've seen the Petersham Hole' were spotted as far away as the Mediterranean.

Farm Lodge and Avenue Lodge on the eastern side of the Petersham Road are two early cottages that may have flanked the stable yard of Montrose House. By the time the land tax returns start in 1780 the two houses were leased out by the Dysarts; Farm Lodge had adjoining stables and Avenue Lodge was occupied by a blacksmith and farrier. The stables were used by bargemen until 1860, at which time there was sufficient stabling for 70 horses. In 1900 a branch of the Richmond Free Library opened at Farm Lodge, though it was presumably not used much as it was closed eight years later.

From about 1900 the old stable yard was used by the Richmond Corporation. Not long after the First World War, Avenue Lodge and its smithy became a motor garage.

In 2003 the Ham and Petersham Association led a vigorous fight against the proposed building development at the rear of the Lodges. As a result the development was considerably reduced in size, to a terrace of four houses and a small office block, and some views of Richmond Park behind the new buildings have been retained.

Above: The blacksmith's forge at the rear of the two Lodges in about 1907, now the Forge Lane development. Photographed by W S Campbell in 1907 for *Rural Nooks round London* by Charles G Harper

Right: Farm Lodge and Avenue Lodge, a pen and ink drawing by Edward Walker from the Recording Britain Collection
©*V&A Images/Victoria and Albert Museum, London*

Opposite: Farm Lodge c.1900 *(reproduced by kind permission of Sir David Williams)* and as it is today

There is an entry in the Petersham Vestry record dated 8th April 1716 which states that a village maypole was ordered to be taken down because it was rotten and dangerous to *'Passengers'*. The maypole probably stood in the open space in front of what is now the Arched Lodge at the entrance to the Petersham Avenue to Ham House. New Lodge, as it was known, was erected by the 9th Earl of Dysart in 1900. It is a neo-Jacobean building of brick with bath stone dressage, designed by R D Oliver; it bears a large Tollemache/Dysart coat of arms and the motto *Confido Conquiesco* (I trust and am content). There is a plaque on the wall at the entrance to Petersham Avenue erected by residents of Petersham in 1977 to commemorate the Queen's Silver Jubilee. Nearby is Tree Close, a development of twelve small houses built in 1976 by Manning, Clamp and Partners for Richmond Churches Housing Trust.

The white-boarded, slate-roofed building on the eastern side of the Fox and Duck public house is the original village watchman's hut and lock-up which was erected in 1787. In the Petersham Vestry and Parish records of that year, it was *'Ordred that Mr Challen* (the Churchwarden) *do put up the Stocks Imediatly by the side of the Pound and Ordred that a stocke House be Erected at the same place & at the same time'*.

The watch house or lock-up served as both a resting-place for the night watchman and as a temporary lock-up for law-breakers. The small walled area in front of the lock-up was the village pound, where stray cattle were held until claimed by their owners.

Parish Councils introduced lock-ups in the late eighteenth century to deal with an increase invagrancy and drunkenness, and nearly every village in the country had its own lock-up. The Parish Constable or watchman, also known as Sergeant of the Night, would be elected each year at the annual vestry meeting of the Parish Council. His was a tough job: highwaymen were frequently active on the Petersham Road at this time, and the watchman was well equipped to deal with them, with his musket, bayonet, pair of pistols, cartridge box, three pounds of grapeshot, powder flask, lantern and a greatcoat to keep him warm throughout the long winter nights.

The Metropolitan Police was formed in 1829 and by the late 1830s the new police had taken over most of the outer areas of London. As new police stations were built lock-ups became redundant, and most were pulled down for development as they were on prime sites in town centres. It is thought that the Petersham lock-up survived as the Council used it as a storeroom for their tools.

In 1940 the old timber-constructed Fox and Duck public house next door, which probably dated from about 1700, was demolished and rebuilt. It is said to have been the last all-timber building in the borough.

In 1955 the survival of the lock-up was again in doubt, as some Petersham villagers felt that it should be demolished on account of its dilapidated state. Fortunately the Ancient Monuments Committee stepped in and decided that it was worth preserving, and Surrey County Council agreed to repairs costing £40. It is now a Grade II listed building, and in 2004, thanks to the representations made by the Environment Trust for Richmond, it was placed on the English Heritage list of important buildings at risk (the BAR register). Further restoration work was needed on both the lock-up and the Pound, and the Ham and Petersham Association succeeded in ensuring that this was carried out, with the help of the Environment Trust and a generous donation from the Historic Buildings Trust.

In Charles D Warren's *History of St Peter's Church* there is an interesting account of some of the duties of the Parish Beadle in 1804, Thomas Painter. He had to *'patrol the river bank during the summer months to prevent bathing during prohibited hours'*, for which he was paid the sum of £1; his main duty was to *'clear the Parish of Beggars and Vagrants'*. William Bennett held the post until his death in 1912 at the age of 86. The inscription on his tombstone at St Peter's Church records that he was *'Beadle of this parish 46 years'*.

The Parish Beadle was provided with a uniform at the expense of the parish. This attained its most imposing and picturesque form in the nineteenth century, when it consisted of a long dark-blue coat adorned with brass buttons and having scarlet cuffs and collar edged with gold braid, a scarlet cape similarly edged, a tall silk hat with a narrow strip of gold braid round the brim and a broad band of the same material fastened at the front by a gilt buckle, and a scarlet-fronted waistcoat with sleeves and brass buttons. In addition he was supplied with trousers, boots and stockings, and with his official staff some five or six feet in length.

'Beating the Bounds' was an ancient tradition throughout the country and an annual event in Ham and Petersham. Its purpose was to ensure that the line of the parish boundary did not get forgotten at a time when there were no maps to form a permanent record. Each year parish officials, accompanied by residents and young boys, and led by a small group of musicians, would together perambulate the route carrying willow wands, rods or poles. At the edges of the parish they would beat the stone posts with their wands to markthe boundary. It was the custom at each major boundary mark for a young boy to be turned upside down and bounced with their heads on the boundary stones so that they remembered where they were!

Where the Thames forms the Petersham boundary, boats were hired to convey parishioners along the middle of the river. Although the ceremony took place on Ascension Day, by the 19th century it had ceased to possess

Right: An early 1900s photograph of a road sweeper on the Petersham Road opposite the old Petersham Post Office
Reproduced by kind permission of Sir David Williams

Right, below: Another early photograph of the Post Office. It occupied a little wooden building by the road in front of Ivy House, now known as Petersham Hollow, and was run by generations of the Long family, including Lydia Maria Long, Petersham's first postmistress. It was destroyed by a bomb in 1941
Reproduced by kind permission of the Local Studies Library, Richmond

Opposite: Myrtle Cottage in 1908 with the Petersham Stores next door, a single-storey shop which was built on in the early 1880s
Reproduced by kind permission of the Local Studies Library, Richmond

Opposite, below: Beadles were dressed to convey an image of importance to the public. The most famous Beadle was of course Mr Bumble in Dickens' Oliver Twist. This picture is taken from *Character Sketches from Dickens* published in 1924. The bicorn hat of the late 18th and early 19th centuries as worn by Mr Bumble, where the wide brim was folded up to form two points, was superseded in the later 19th century by the top hat, tall and cylindrical with a narrow brim, made of silk plush. The old uniform and bicorn worn by the Petersham Beadle are now at the Richmond Museum, though sadly not on permanent display

any religious significance it may have had, and had become a secular custom. It ceased altogether in 1850, rendered unnecessary by the publication of the Ordnance Survey maps.

Whorne's Place is a re-creation by the American architect Blunden Shadbolt of a house by the same name which was built in about 1487 at Cuxton, near Rochester, for Sir William Whorne, then Lord Mayor of London. Shadbolt dismantled it in 1928 and used the salvaged medieval materials to re-erect it on this site in Petersham. It was known as the Old House until the 1980s.

Above: Whorne's Place with the iconic clipped elephant hedges

Right: Gort Lodge on Sudbrook Lane

Opposite, top: Tony Rampton's 1965 oil on canvas of Miss Julius in her stout walking boots on Sudbrook Lane where she lived at 'The Cottage'; by all accounts she was quite a character. The Rampton family lived at Gort Lodge for many years; and top right the same view today

Opposite, middle left: Gort House, said to have been built in c.1774 although Pevsner describes it as early 18th century. Originally it was one house with Gort Lodge

Opposite, middle right: Cecil House which dates from 1767-80, from land left by George Cole in 1624, then Lord of the Manor

Opposite below: A view of All Saints church showing the bronze figure of Christ on top of the 118 ft campanile

Elm Cottage, now called Elm Lodge, is an early Georgian house which once had large gardens, stables, a cowshed and fields and an orchard standing in a plot of about 3.5 acres. In 1817 Sir Henry Charles Englefield (see notes) bought the property and left it in his will to J E Strickland in 1824; he granted a lease to the Hon William Robert Spencer (see notes). His father, Lord Charles Spencer, who was the brother of the 4th Duke of Marlborough, died in 1820 whilst staying with his son and was buried in St Peter's churchyard at his own desire.

Charles Dickens (1812–70) rented the property for four months in the summer of 1839. His diary entry for Tuesday 30 April reads: *'Took possession of Elm Cottage, Petersham for 4 months – rent for term £100.'* At this time Dickens's wife Catherine was pregnant with their third child; Kate was born on 29 October of that year. It seems that they also lived at Woodbine Cottage or Park Cottage on the Petersham Road for a few months three years earlier.

It is believed that Dickens wrote most of *Nicholas Nickleby* (serialised between April 1838 and October 1839) at Elm Cottage. The quarrel between Sir Mulberry Hawk and Lord Frederick Verisopht on their return from the Hampton races led to a duel which took place on Ham Fields: *'Shall we join the company in the avenue of trees which leads from Petersham to Ham House, and settle the exact spot when we arrive there? . . . they at length turned to the right, and taking a track across a little meadow, passed Ham House and came into some fields beyond. In one of these they stopped.'*

Dickens wrote, in a letter to his friend the artist Daniel Maclise, who also contributed many illustrations to Dickens' works (see notes): *'. . . have only sense and energy sufficient to say 'Come down – come down, revive yourself with country air – and that without loss of time . . . . I'll warrant you good health for 12 months at least . . . . the roads about are jewelled after dusk with glow-worms, the leaves are all out and the flowers too, swimming feats from Petersham to Richmond Bridge have been achieved before breakfast, I myself have risen at 6 and plunged head foremost into the water to the astonishment and admiration of all beholders . . . .'*

His friend and biographer, John Forster, in his *Life of Charles Dickens* wrote: *'. . . . at Petersham, where extensive garden-grounds admitted of much athletic competition, from the more difficult forms of which I in general modestly retired, but where Dickens for the most part held his own against even such accomplished athletes as Maclise and Mr. Beard. Bar-leaping, bowling, and quoits, were among the games carried on with the greatest ardour; and in sustained energy, or what is called keeping it up, Dickens certainly distanced every competitor. Even the lighter recreations of battledore and bagatelle were pursued with relentless activity; and at such amusements as the Petersham races, in those days rather celebrated, and which he visited daily while they lasted, he worked much harder himself than the running horses did.'*

Margaret Mary Julia (Daisy) Ashford (1881–1972), the celebrated child author, was born at Elm Lodge, the home of her paternal grandmother and of her aunt Julia Ashford, on 7 April 1881. The family soon moved to Parkgate in Petersham before moving to Lewes in Sussex where Daisy wrote *The Young Visiters* in 1890. The book was not published until 1919, when it immediately became a publishing phenomenon, being reprinted 18 times in the year of publication.

In the 1890s Elm Lodge was an exclusive private school run by a Miss Holland: the fees were £2 2s per term in 1893 rising to £3 15s in 1895. In 1902 the house was bought by the Dysarts and sold in the 1949 Ham and Petersham estate auction. In 1964 3.5 acres of the 5 acres of grounds were sold for development, and eight new houses were built in a new road appropriately called Dickens Close.

Opposite: A photograph of Daisy Ashford, author of *The Young Visiters*, in 1919

This page: Two photos of Elm Lodge, and Charles Dickens in 1827 aged 27 from a painting by his friend the artist Daniel Maclise

Sudbrook Park, an elegant and remarkable building near the Richmond Park boundary, was originally the home of John Campbell (1680–1743), 2nd Duke of Argyll, later Duke of Greenwich; he was the grandson of Elizabeth, 2nd Countess of Dysart, and was born at Ham House. Its name is taken from the Sudbrook (meaning South Brook) which was a small stream rising in what is now Richmond Park and running through Sudbrook Park and Petersham to the Thames to the west of River Lane. The surname 'de Sudbrooke' is found in Petersham as early as 1211 and occurs frequently in the 13th and 14th centuries.

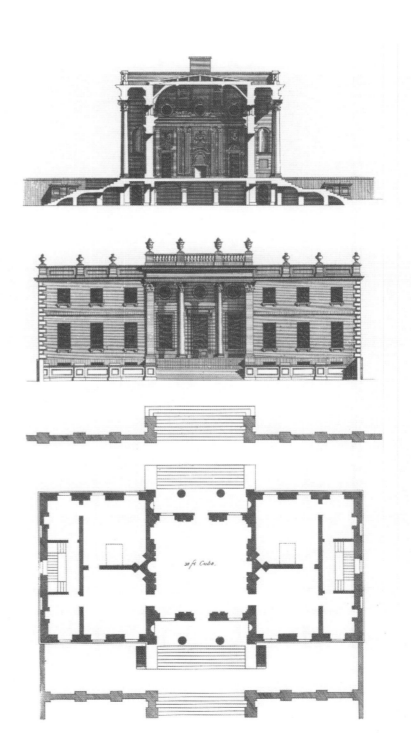

The Duke bought 20 acres in the Petersham Field in 1712 and Hatch Court (see page 55) and its grounds in 1715. To these he was able to add 30 acres of Richmond Park, granted to him by King George I in 1715, and he commissioned James Gibbs, a friend and disciple of Sir Christopher Wren, to build him a mansion of white Portland stone and dark red brick. Gibbs was one of the most important English architects in the 18th century; among his most famous buildings are the Radcliffe Library in Oxford and St Mary-le-Strand and St Martins-in-the-Fields in London. Sudbrook is regarded as an important and rare example of Gibbs's more domestic architectural achievements, and one of the best examples of English Palladian architecture. The original plan of the house has a strictly symmetrical layout, with identical porticos on the south and north fronts. There is a large centrally placed room, the ornate 30 foot Cube Room, one of the great features of the interior, with smaller rooms leading from it.

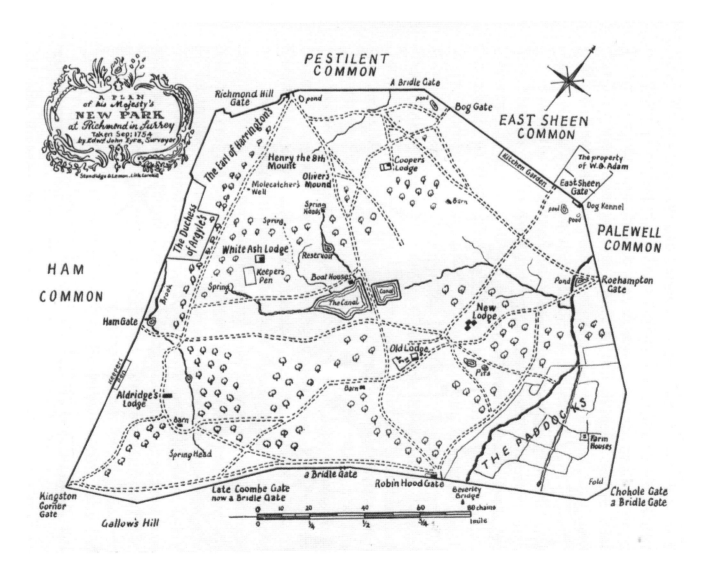

The Duke was an eminent military commander, serving with great distinction under the Duke of Marlborough. He is described by Lady Louisa Stuart as possessing: *'a personal beauty, an expressive countenance, a commanding air and the most easy engaging gracefulness of manner'*. And he was immortalised by Alexander Pope:
'Argyll, the state's whole thunder born to wield
And shake alike the senate and the field.'

The Duke's first marriage to Mary Brown was not successful, and after her death in 1717 he married Jane Warburton, a maid of honour to Queen Anne and to Caroline, Princess of Wales. Although belonging to an old Cheshire family, she lacked refinement and her frank admiration for the Duke, which was the source of much amusement at Court, had, in fact, proved the origin of the courtship. Throughout his life he remained, according to Lady Louisa Stuart, *'a faithful, doating and adoring husband'*. However, he desperately wanted a son and heir and in this he was disappointed. The Duke and Duchess had five daughters, one of whom died in infancy.

The entrance to the mansion is at the end of Sudbrook Lane, through an arched lodge, where the magnificent Palladian building comes into view. The annex on the right of the house known as 'The Young Ladies House' was built by the Duke, probably in the 1720s, for his daughters, who were variously nicknamed the *'Bawling Campbells'* or the *'Screaming Sisterhood'* because of their loud and shrill voices. It seems that the girls' education was not considered of great importance as it would have been if they were sons. The Duke stipulated only that there was no need for them to learn French because *'one language was enough for a woman to talk in'*; they seem to have had little formal education of any kind and were allowed to do as they pleased.

The Duke died at Sudbrook in 1743 and was buried at Westminster Abbey. The inscription on his monument reads: *'In memory of an honest man, a constant friend, John the Great Duke of Argyll and Greenwich, a General and orator, excelled by none in the age he lived'.*

As he had no male heirs, his brother Archibald Campbell, the Earl of Islay, succeeded to the Argyll titles and estates. The Duke left Sudbrook Park to his eldest daughter Caroline, giving his wife the Dowager Duchess of Argyll use of it in her lifetime. In fact she spent much of her time there until her death in 1767. Caroline (1717–94) was born at Sudbrook and baptised at St Peter's Church. She married firstly Francis Scott, Earl of Dalkeith. He died of smallpox when Caroline was five months pregnant with their sixth child. Her second marriage was to Charles Townshend (see Ormeley Lodge page 52). Walpole observed of this marriage: *'Townshend marries the great Dowager Dalkeith. His parts and presumption are prodigious . . .'* On the death of her widowed mother Caroline was created Baroness Greenwich, and she resided at Sudbrook until her death in 1794; she was buried alongside her father in the Argyll family vault at Westminster Abbey.

Lady Caroline was the only sister to have children. Lady Anne, the second daughter and beauty, married Lord Strafford at an early age; she suffered from epileptic fits, then known as 'the falling sickness'. The third daughter Elizabeth, Lady Betty as she was known, married her cousin James Stuart Mackenzie (see Bute House, page 96). The youngest Campbell sister Lady Mary (1727–1811) married Edward, Viscount Coke, son of the Earl of Leicester of Holkham Hall, Norfolk. The marriage was not a success; it took place in 1747, when she was just nineteen. They separated after just two years, plunging the two families into litigation. A settlement was reached on condition that Lady Mary resided with her mother at Sudbrook and never visited London. Her freedom was restored, however, on the death of her husband in 1753.

Lady Mary Coke was said to have a temperament which made her the object of contempt and ridicule. Her fearless prattle as a child entertained her father, who made her his favourite, and it seemed that this was to the detriment of her future disposition. She also had the famous Tollemache temper and had a high opinion of her own prerogatives and merits. Much of what is known about her stems from her letters and journals, written mostly at Sudbrook between 1766 and 1774. She was a keen gardener and loved to play cards. It was also said that she was devoted to Edward, Duke of York and Albany, the younger brother of the future King George III.

On the death of Lady Greenwich the ownership of Sudbrook passed to her son, Henry Scott (1746–1812), 3rd Duke of Buccleuch (see Montagu House, page 74), and then eighteen years later to his son Charles, the fourth Duke, who died in 1819, when the property was sold by auction for the benefit of his daughters.

A later tenant was the Earl of Durham, one of the authors of the Great Reform Act of 1832, and it is said that an early draft of the Act was made at Sudbrook. In the mid-1800s a Hydropathic Spa took over the house, part of a faddish craze at that time for the 'water cure' which involved constant soaking under cold showers

and wrapping the body in wet sheets, as well as drinking pints of cold water. This was led at first by Dr Weiss of Vienna and then from 1844/5 by James Ellis, a lace merchant from Twickenham trained by both Vincent Preissnitz and C von Schlemmer (see page 62). Although he called himself a doctor, he was not recognised as a physician in England. In 1844 *The Times* reported that Sir Francis Burdett MP had died after Ellis had advised on hydropathy treatment for his gout. In 1846 he stood trial for manslaughter at the Central Criminal Court in London after the death of another of his patients, Richard Dresser, but was acquitted. Despite these setbacks Ellis remained at Sudbrook until 1879.

The Crown repurchased the freehold in 1853, and has held it since then. In 1886 the house became a private hotel, and the Richmond Golf Club, established in 1891, took over the lease in 1898; before moving to Sudbrook they had used the Fox and Duck public house for changing facilities and as a clubroom. The famous Cube Room is now the club members' dining hall.

Opposite: The north front of Sudbrook Park; this page, views of the south front of the mansion

Vincent van Gogh, one of the greatest post-impressionist painters, was born in Holland in 1853. His father was a Protestant pastor of the Dutch Reformed Church in southern Holland. Before he took up art seriously at the age of 27 he spent some time in England, and in 1876 he was a young student assisting a Congregational minister, the Revd Slade Jones of Isleworth, who ran a small boarding school at Isleworth and held meetings and services at a church in Turnham Green, Chiswick. Van Gogh was employed to teach and supervise the pupils at the school and collect school fees. It seems that he also helped Mr Jones as a lay preacher at Turnham Green, Richmond and Petersham. He walked, probably from Turnham Green, to the chapel at Petersham, and conducted a service there. On returning home he wrote of the events of the day to his brother Theo and also made this sketch below. In the summer of 1879 the Belgian Protestant Church decided that van Gogh was not a suitable person for evangelical work on the grounds that he could not preach very well. Fortunately, his skills as a painter were soon to prove to be of a very different order.

Above: The Wesleyan Methodist chapel, Petersham, by Vincent van Gogh, 1876.
Courtesy of the Stedilijk Museum, Amsterdam
A small wooden building with a corrugated iron roof, this chapel was built in 1866 at the end of a short lane which ran beside the Victorian villa known as 'The Poplars', now 291 Petersham Road. It is shown on Ordnance Survey maps of 1869 and 1884, and was demolished in 1891

Right: Petersham saw its first high-tech German prefabricated HUF home in 2008, called Twyntre

Douglas House was built in the early 1700s. It was originally known as Hall Place or Petersham Place, the name Douglas House only appearing in the 1890s. The house is set in spacious grounds and has an attractive semi-circular approach. A stable block is set at right angles to the house at the side. It came into the possession of Henry Boyle, Lord Carlton in 1717 and he bequeathed the house in 1728 to his nephew Charles Douglas, 3rd Duke of Queensberry. Charles Douglas married Catherine 'Kitty' Hyde, one of the noted beauties of her time and the second daughter of the 2nd Earl of Rochester (see Old Petersham Lodge, page 80). The couple, who were second cousins, were said to be devoted. The Duke had inherited great wealth and was a quiet, patient man and a natural diplomat. His wife had strong opinions and had no hesitation in voicing them.

She hated artifice and rarely wore jewellery, often appearing in court in the simplest of clothes, as shown in the above portrait. Pope wrote of her:
'Since Queensberry to strip there's no compelling
'tis from a handmaid we must take our Helen'.

The Duke and Duchess acted as hosts to the literary and art world, and one such guest was John Gay (1685–1732), the playwright. It is said that he wrote the very successful *Beggar's Opera* in 1728 at Petersham, in the Queensberrys' summerhouse by the river. Lady Mary Coke describes in her journals a visit to the Duke and Duchess of Queensberry, when the Duchess showed her a summer house *'which is indeed very whimsical; one of the rooms is 30 ft long and but 7 ft high, the other is the same length and 11 ft in height'.*

Gay had been secretary to Lord Clarendon and later also attracted patronage from the Duke and Duchess, who found him a small sinecure. In 1729 Gay was refused a licence for *Polly*, his sequel to the *Beggar's Opera*. The Duchess took up his cause, quarrelled with the Lord Chamberlain, offended King George II and was ordered to withdraw from Court, which she did but returned in 1747. At one time she also had an altercation with her neighbour at Petersham, the 4th Earl of Dysart, about a piece of land between Douglas House and Ham House.

The Duke and Duchess had two sons; the elder, Lord Drumlanrig, seems to have committed suicide at the age of 31, apparently suffering from depression. Their younger son died soon after of tuberculosis. After the deaths of Catherine Duchess of Queensberry in 1777 (according to Horace Walpole 'from a surfeit of cherries'), and her husband the Duke the following year, Douglas House was inherited first by their unmarried niece Lady Jane Scott (1723–79), sister of the Earl of Dalkeith, and then by Lady Jane's niece, Lady Frances Scott, the posthumous daughter of the Earl of Dalkeith and his wife, Caroline Campbell, later Baroness Greenwich, of Sudbrook Park. Lady Frances (see notes) married Archibald Douglas in 1783 as his second wife, and he was created Baron Douglas in 1790. Lady Frances' daughter Caroline Lucy inherited the house in 1817. She had married Captain (later Vice Admiral Sir) George Scott in 1810. Lady Caroline Lucy Scott (1784–1857) was a novelist and author of *Trevelyan*. She was also an accomplished amateur artist (see page 16).

Opposite: A watercolour of Douglas House by John Wykeham Archer, dated 1849, showing a later wing added to the rear of the original Queen Anne house
© *Trustees of the British Museum, London*

Above: Douglas House in its present role as part of the German School

Though she and her husband continued to live in Douglas House, Lady Caroline Scott made over part ownership in 1827 to her younger brother James (who had taken holy orders and succeeded to the title as the 4th Baron Douglas in 1848). They both died in 1857 and their youngest sister Mary Sidney Douglas inherited the property. It then passed through her to the Drummond-Moray family.

In 1971 the house passed out of private ownership when it was bought by the Federal Republic of Germany for use as a German school for the children of its nationals living in the United Kingdom. The partnership Kersten Martinoff Struhk won an architectural competition in Germany for the development, modern school buildings were constructed, and the school opened in 1981. Douglas House was preserved for use as offices and the head's residence. The stable block was converted to extra classrooms and over the years additional school buildings have been added in the grounds.

The Douglas House Meadow which leads down to the river is the home of the Petersham and Ham Sea Scouts, one of the oldest scout groups still in existence, which celebrated its centenary in 2008.

Polo was first established in the area in 1926. The 'Stick and Ball Field' was originally the Ham House orchard and was cleared of the old apple trees by George Stevens in 1954. He farmed the area known as Manor Farm which had been leased from the Dysart estate. In 1965 a fire destroyed the original clubhouse but soon the members had purchased and re-erected an old army Nissen hut from the wartime barracks in Richmond Park which, although slightly modified, is still used as the clubhouse today. In 1970 the club purchased the freehold of the land from Stevens's family, so providing Ham and Petersham with a permanently dedicated polo ground for the first time.

Our tour of Ham and Petersham is now complete, and the question arises what lessons for the future can be learnt from it. First surely is the importance of historical awareness and vigilance by residents and others when new developments are being considered. The sad saga of Ham Manor Farm must never be repeated. Secondly the accumulated experience of the Ham and Petersham Association in articulating local opinion and expressing it in the right quarters has been proved vital, and must be maintained. Thirdly, while ensuring the preservation and judicious enhancement of the beautiful buildings and open spaces our predecessors have left us, we should not seek to turn the villages into museum pieces.

To maintain a lively environment and society some new developments are needed; but if these are too many, the essential rural spirit would be gradually extinguished. With the right balance achieved here, we can bequeath to our successors an even more beautiful and varied mixture of old and new than the one we ourselves inherited.

This varied collection of supplementary information starts with items which apply to the book as a whole, or to several different sections. These are followed by items which apply primarily to one section, which are grouped by page number.

General sources and recommendations for further reading

The *Oxford Dictionary of National Biography,* freely available online to local library members in Richmond and many other places in the UK.

Palaces and Parks of Richmond and Kew. 2 vols., John Cloake, Phillimore & Co., 1995 and 1996. The chapters on Richmond Park are particularly relevant to this book.

A History of Richmond Park. C L Collenette, Sidgwick & Jackson, 1937.

Richmond Park. Michael Baxter Brown, Robert Hale, 1985

History and Antiquities of Richmond, Kew, Petersham and Ham. E Beresford Chancellor, 1894.

The Buildings of England, London 2: South. Bridget Cherry and Nikolaus Pevsner, Yale University Press, London and New Haven, Connecticut, 1983. Originally published by Penguin Books in 1983.

The Walker's Guide: the Thames, Hampton to Richmond Bridge. David McDowall, 2002.

Ham and Petersham as it was. James Green and Silvia Greenwood on behalf of the Richmond Society History Section, 1980.

Bygone Richmond. H M Cundall, John Lane, the Bodley Head, 1925.

Views on the Thames and Medway. William Tombleson, London, 1833–1834.

Ham House and its owners through five centuries 1610–2006. Evelyn Pritchard, Richmond Local History Society, 2007 (based on a shorter version with a different title first published in 1995).

Guide to the street names of Ham and Petersham. Evelyn Pritchard, edited and augmented by Leonard Chave, Richmond Local History Society, 2005.

The growth of Richmond. John Cloake, Richmond Local History Society Paper, second revised edition, 2003.

Ham and Petersham at 2000. Leonard Chave (ed), Ham Amenities Group, 2000.
This book gives an excellent and wide-ranging account of life in Ham and Petersham at the turn of the century, covering for example education, health, employment, transport, wildlife, shopping and sport, as well as history and geography. It will be an invaluable source for future historians.

The growth of Ham in the 20th century (I): the battle for Ham's green acres. Leonard Chave, Journal of Richmond Local History Society, no.26, 2005.

The growth of Ham in the 20th century (II): bricks, mortar and open spaces. Leonard Chave, Journal of Richmond Local History Society, no.27, 2006.

A portrait of Ham in early Victorian times 1840–1860. Evelyn Pritchard, Alma Publishers, 1999.

Richmond. Kathleen Courlander, Batsford, 1953.

The London Encyclopaedia. Ben Weinreb and Christopher Hibbert (eds), third revised edition, Pan Macmillan, 2008.

Greater London: a narrative of its history, its people and its places, Vol. II. Edward Walford, Cassell, 1883.

House names

Houses did not generally have their own names until the arrival of the first Penny Post in 1840. Before that time they were usually referred to by the name of the current owner or occupier. For clarity, the present-day names of houses have normally been used in the text.

Evelyn Pritchard and Silvia Greenwood

There are no less than 20 boxes of original papers belonging to these two past residents of Ham at the Local Studies Library at the Old Town Hall in Richmond town centre. They both contributed much to what we know about Petersham and especially Ham through their painstaking research, and the book owes a great deal to them both.

Evelyn Pritchard lived in Ham for 50 years. She worked as a scientist in the paper and printing trade and on her retirement became a diligent and much-respected local historian.

Silvia Greenwood's great-grandfather came to Ham Common in 1830, at the time that St Andrew's Church was being built and the village horse races were still held on the Common. He was a member of the Ham Common Prosecution Defence Committee formed in 1891 to protect the rights of the villagers from the enclosure of waste and common land by the Dysart family. Her grandfather Cornelius Greenwood first worked as a ploughman and two of his sons became market gardeners, growing flowers and vegetables on and around the Lammas Lands, now Ham Lands. Another son kept a dairy on the Upper Ham Road next to the Gate House, grazing his cattle on the common land by St Andrew's Church. Her father Fred became a master plumber and was very knowledgeable about the large houses in the area where he worked, including Ham House. This was an interest that he shared with his daughter.

Marjorie Lansdale produced a charming booklet entitled *Ham and Petersham Reminiscences* which was published by the then Ham and Petersham Ratepayers' & Residents' Association in 1983. Marjorie was actively involved in the work of the Ham and Petersham Association from its earliest years until her sad death in 1993. She held a succession of offices over the years and eventually became Vice-president. The Lansdales lived at Rose Cottage, now the site of a large modern house north of Forbes House on the south-west side of Ham Common. Marjorie's family have generously allowed us the use of several extracts from her reminiscences, which cover the years 1922 to 1983.

Recording Britain Collection

The brainchild of Sir Kenneth Clark, this scheme was set up at the beginning of the Second World War to employ artists to record in watercolours and drawings the country's scenes and landscapes that were considered to be under threat from bomb damage or invasion. Funded by the Pilgrim Trust (a fund provided by the American millionaire Edward Harkness), it includes many scenes of traditional country life and rural industries in decline at the time. In 1949, the Pilgrim Trust presented the pictures to the Victoria and Albert Museum and they can now be seen on request in the Prints and Drawings Study Room. There are no less than 40 images of Ham and Petersham, including rural scenes and house paintings drawn in 1941 by Wilfred Fairclough, John Sanderson-Wells, Edward Walker and George W. Hooper. Some of them were published in *Recording Britain* Vol. 1, Arnold Palmer (ed), Oxford University Press, 1946. We have reproduced a number of them: in Ham on pages 17, 19, 22, 27 and 31; and in Petersham on pages 93 and 103.

Notes and sources relating to individual topics and illustrations

Title pages and Introduction

Photo of the entrance to Ham House
© David Yates 2009.

The picture on the title verso page is the same as the one on the front cover of the Earl of Rochester's house, New Park (Old Petersham Lodge). It is attributed to Adriæn van Diest c.1700–1705 © Yale Center for British Art, Paul Mellon collection, New Haven, Connecticut. It is also reproduced on page 68 and the caption here also gives details of the houses that are depicted in the painting. There are two other notable early oil paintings of the view from Richmond Hill of interest because they face towards Ham and Petersham. The earliest, by Jan Siberechts, painted in 1677, depicts the area before the building of New Park. It shows extensive flooding of the Thames, before it had been properly embanked. The other painting in about 1720 is by Leonard Knyff and is reproduced on page 9.

Page 6

John Rocque (c.1704–1762) was born in France of a Huguenot family which moved to Geneva after fleeing France, before settling in London. He was a land surveyor and cartographer, one of the most prolific and innovative map-makers of the 18th century. His renowned maps of London and its environs were surveyed from 1738 and published in twenty-four sheets in 1746.

Page 7

Although lampreys do not seem to be mentioned anywhere else in the Domesday Book, eels formed an important part of the dues paid to the landowner in many riverside districts. Until the first Teddington Lock was built in 1811 and restricted their movements, they would have come upstream from Richmond to Kingston and beyond in large shoals in the early summer. This migration was known to the Surrey and Middlesex fishermen as the celebrated Eel Fair. Eels were a great delicacy and eel-pie a favourite dish. They are now virtually extinct on the river.

Pages 9 – 10

The fight for the view from Richmond Hill. Ron Berryman, Journal of Richmond Local History Society, no.21, 2000.
Saving the view from Richmond Hill. Ron Berryman, Journal of Richmond Local History Society, no.22, 2001. These two articles by Ron Berryman give an excellent account of the ten years it took to arrive at a settlement which resulted in the 1902 Richmond, Petersham and Ham Open Spaces Act.

The need for a rural idyll: preserving the view from Richmond Hill. Anne Milton-Worssell, Journal of Richmond Local History Society, no.24, 2003.

The English peasantry and the enclosure of common fields. Gilbert Slater, Constable, 1907.

The court baron was authorised by the King and presided over by the Lords of the Manor. It mainly dealt with matters relating to the duties and services owed by the serfs or peasants to the Lords of the Manor. The court leet had extra powers to those of the court baron. It was a Recording Court granted to the borough of Richmond by the Kings Charter. Among the duties of the court leet were 'to enquire regularly and periodically into the proper condition of watercourses, roads, paths and ditches; to guard against all manner of encroachments upon the public rights, whether by unlawful enclosure or otherwise, and to preserve landmarks'.

Ham

Page 11

The 'CABAL' Ministry – Clifford, Ashley, Buckingham, Arlington and Lauderdale – formed the inner Cabinet advising Charles II in the late 1660s and early 1670s.

Photo of the garden front of Ham House
© David Yates 2009.

Page 14

Ham House Guide Books, published by The National Trust.

John Evelyn's Journal 1678, vol. IV, p.143.
This extract is often slightly misquoted, probably because of reliance on readily available 19th century transcriptions.

Richmond and its surrounding scenery. Barbara Hofland, 1832.

The Rampton family kindly allowed us to reproduce this painting by Tony Rampton and also the one on page 109.

Pages 15 – 17

The diary and correspondence of Ralph Thoresby, 1712; vol. 2 p.13, ed. J Hunter, 1830. Ralph Thoresby (1658–1725) was a noted antiquary and topographer from Leeds. He kept a diary for most of his adult life, recording his travels and observations.

The origin of the Ham House grounds. John Cloake, Journal of Richmond Local History Society, no.22, 2001.

Arcadian Thames: the river landscape from Hampton to Kew. Mavis Batey, Henrietta Buttery, David Lambert and Kim Wilkie. Barn Elms Publishing, 1994.

Ham Avenues Restoration Management Plan. Kim Wilkie and Associates, 2002.

Ham House Guide Books, published by The National Trust.

Ham House and its owners through five centuries 1610–2006. Evelyn Pritchard, Richmond Local History Society, 2007 (based on a shorter version with a different title first published in 1995).

The early history of Ham, Part I. John Cloake, Journal of Richmond Local History Society, no.10, 1990.

The early history of Ham, Part II. John Cloake, Journal of Richmond Local History Society, no.11, 1991.

The drawing by John Constable RA, dated 1834, was given to the Victoria and Albert Museum by his daughter Isobel. It is entitled *The Avenue of trees at Ham*. On the reverse is another pencil drawing by Constable, *A woman by an old Willow Tree at Ham, Surrey* (see page 135). They are in the Prints and Drawings Study Room at the Museum.

Page 18 Ham Lands and the ferry

Ham Lands: a guide to nature conservation. London Borough of Richmond upon Thames, 1987.

The ferry from Ham to Twickenham. T H R Cashmore, Journal of Richmond Local History Society, no.25, 2004.

Pages 20 – 23 the Manor House, Ham

The London Encyclopaedia. Ben Weinreb and Christopher Hibbert (eds), London, 1986.

Letters from Sir Everard Home to his midshipman son, later Captain Sir James Everard Home R N; copies in the possession of Mr E R A de Unger. After Sir Everard's death in 1832 he left the Manor House to this son, who lived there, between commissions in South East Asia, until the early 1840s, when the costs of maintaining the house became too much for him; the house was finally sold in the late 1840s.

Flooding events from the online *Chronology of British Hydrological Events* via the British Hydrological Society website, see www.dundee.ac.uk/geography/cbhe

Sir George Gilbert Scott (1811–1878), Architect of the Gothic Revival. Victoria and Albert Museum Exhibition Catalogue, September 1978. Also other papers in the possession of Mr E R A de Unger.

Pages 24 – 25 Beaufort House

The owners of Beaufort House kindly provided a copy of their House History, compiled by Peter Bushell.

One particular girl who attended the Catholic school at Beaufort House in 1861 was Marian Emma Chase, who was to become a well-known botanical water colourist. In 1888 the Royal Botanical Society awarded her a silver medal for one of her drawings.

After the Great Fire of London in 1666, insurance companies started to offer cover, on payment of a premium, against loss by fire. In the 18th and 19th centuries, before the days of the municipal fire service,

Firemarks were introduced to distinguish between the different insurance offices. Embossed with the sign of the company, they were put up on the front of the insured building and served as a form of advertisement. The companies often started their own fire brigades and also sometimes employed the Thames Watermen to act as part-time firemen. It was not unheard of for fire fighters to refuse to put a fire out if they could not see their specific Firemark on the building.

Pages 26 – 27 Newman House

Cardinal Newman and his boyhood in Ham. Stephen Pasmore, Journal of Richmond Local History Society, no.16, 1995. The letter quoted was written to a Miss Holmes in 1861.

Page 28 Queen Charlotte's letter

Although it has been claimed that it was Selby House on Ham Common that Queen Charlotte visited, it could also have been Grove House (now Newman House). The Lady Caroline mentioned could have been the unmarried daughter of Joseph Damer, Earl of Dorchester. Mrs Damer may be the well-known sculptress, Anne Seymour (née Conway, 1749–1828) and widow of the Hon. John Damer, Lady Caroline's brother. Mrs Damer was a great friend of Horace Walpole and on his death he bequeathed her Strawberry Hill. She was also an intimate of Mary Berry in whose *The Journals and Correspondence of Mary Berry* the letter from Queen Charlotte is included.

Pages 28 – 31 Ham Street

Pigot's Directory of 1840, *The Post Office Directory* of 1871, and *Kelly's Directory*, 1895, 1937 and 1948 list the residents and commercial establishments of Ham in these years, with varying degrees of completeness.

Not just a pretty face: the story of some cottages in Ham. Celia Nelson, 2007.

Page 32 Selby House

Information taken from Evelyn Pritchard's and Silvia Greenwood's papers, Richmond Local Studies Library.

Pages 33 – 37 Ham Common

An autumn ramble on Ham Common. The Pall Mall Budget Magazine, 1891.

Richmond and its surrounding scenery. Barbara Hofland, 1832, p.33. She was married to the artist Thomas Christopher Hofland (1777–1843).

Ham Common and the Dysarts. William H Harland, 1892.

The defence of Ham Common, with its little-known champion W H Harland. Jackie E M Latham, Journal of Richmond Local History Society, no.24, 2003.

History of St Peter's Church, Petersham. Charles D Warren, Sidgwick & Jackson, 1938. Churchwardens and Churchwardens' Accounts, 'Extra Watching during Ham Fair', p.111.

Ham and Petersham as it was. James Green and Silvia Greenwood on behalf of the Richmond Society History Section, 1980.

One hundred and seventy not out: a history of Ham and Petersham Cricket Club 1815–1985, by Peter Philpot. Geoff Bond, secretary of the Ham and Petersham Cricket Club, kindly provided further historical material about the club.

Celia Nelson's booklet *Not just a pretty face: the story of some cottages in Ham* listed above includes an account of the career and family of the cricketer William Brockwell.

The Ham Pond Story. David Yates for the Ham Pond Working Group, 2002.

The photos of a frosty morning on Ham Common on p.35, nesting swans and riders on horseback p.36, and Ham Pond in winter p.37 are © David Yates 2009.

Page 38 The Little House

The Little House (formerly 'Ivycroft') Ham Common and its association with Miss Hesba Stretton, 1832–1911, a nineteenth century literary figure. Silvia Greenwood, Journal of Richmond Local History Society, no.1, 1981.

Pages 39 – 42 Gordon House, Forbes House and Langham House

A brief history of Gordon, Forbes and Langham Houses on Ham Common. Evelyn Pritchard, Journal of Richmond Local History Society, no.14, 1993.

Pages 42 – 43 Hobarts

Letters of Horace Walpole, 4th Earl of Orford, in nine volumes. Peter Cunningham (ed), John Grant, Edinburgh, 1906. The particular letters quoted are from 1781 vol. viii p.65 and 1791 vol. ix p.325.

Pages 44 – 45 Cassel Hospital

The site of the Cassel Hospital. Evelyn Pritchard, Journal of Richmond Local History Society, no.15, 1994.

The deeds of the Cassel Hospital site, deposited by West Heath School at the Richmond Local Studies Library.

Pages 48 – 49 St Andrew's Church

Saint Andrew's Church, Ham Common, Visitors' Guide.

Kip Waddell, the Church Archivist, his wife Sue, and the present vicar, the Revd Simon Brocklehurst, gave valuable help with some of this information.

The history of St Andrew's Church, Ham Common. Silvia Greenwood. Journal of Richmond Local History Society, no.3, 1982.

Anthony Frederick Blunt served in MI5 during the Second World War. He was a distinguished art historian and Surveyor of the Queen's Pictures, knighted in 1956, exposed as a long-term Soviet spy in 1979 and stripped of his knighthood. He died in 1983. His family lived at Pond House on Ham Common.

Pages 48 – 50 Latchmere House

Camp 020, MI5 and the Nazi spies (Secret History Files). Oliver Hoare (ed), National Archives, 2000.

Page 51 Park Gate House

Palaces and Parks of Richmond and Kew Vol 1. John Cloake, Phillimore & Co., 1995 and 1996.

Charles William de la Poer Beresford (1846–1919), second son of the 4th Marquess of Waterford, was a colourful personality of his day who courted publicity. He was an MP, a dashing sportsman and a courageous and distinguished naval officer. Fondly known by the public as 'Charlie B', he joined the Royal Navy in 1859 and became a rear-admiral in 1897 and a full admiral in 1906. He was a friend of and aide-de-camp to the Prince of Wales (later Edward VII). Interestingly he had a very bitter and public dispute with the First Sea Lord Sir John Fisher (who was his neighbour on Ham Common) over naval reforms.

Brothers William and Edmund started the Vestey family firm in the late 1800s. They made their fortune from importing firstly canned then refrigerated fresh meat in the late 1800s. In the 1900s their empire had expanded to include the retail butcher chain of shops J H Dewhurst, becoming one of the largest privately owned conglomerates in the world.

Pages 52 – 55 Ormeley Lodge

Country Homes, gardens old and new, Petersham, Surrey and its houses II: Ormeley Lodge and Petersham House. Arthur T Bolton, *Country Life*, 26 October 1918.

Some information on the history of Ormeley Lodge is from the unpublished papers of Stephen Pasmore, by kind permission of his daughter.

Page 55 Hatch Court

The National Archives, E36/169 p.707.

The Robin Hood Lands, the Hamlet of Hatch and the Manor of Kingston Canbury. John Cloake, Journal of Richmond Local History Society, no.27, 2006

Page 56 Sudbrook Lodge

Sudbrook Lodge. Stephen Pasmore, Journal of Richmond Local History Society, no.14, 1993.

Pages 60 – 63 South Lodge

Radical Ham Common: some early Victorian visitors. Jackie E M Latham, Journal of Richmond Local History Society, no.23, 2002.

Hydropathy at Ham. Jackie E M Latham, Journal of Richmond Local History Society, no.19, 1998.

Search for a New Eden: James Pierrepont Greaves (1777–1842), the sacred socialist and his followers. Jackie E M Latham, Fairleigh Dickinson University Press and Eurospan, 2000.

Pages 64 – 65 Hardwicke House and Emily Eden

Information on Hardwicke House was kindly supplied by the current owners, including notes on Thomas Tryon from a tercentenary dinner held in 1988 to launch the Anniversary Project, which encouraged house owners to celebrate some past event relating to their house or its contents in the interests of conservation. Further information on Thomas Tryon is given in Stephen Pasmore's article on Sudbrook Lodge, see above.

Emily Eden and her little cottage at Ham Common. Jackie E M Latham, Journal of Richmond Local History Society, no.23, 2002.

Heaven's Command: an Imperial Progress. Jan Morris, Faber and Faber, 1973.

Pages 65 – 66 St Michael's Convent

The history of St Michael's Convent, Ham Common. Evelyn Pritchard, Journal of Richmond Local History Society, no.16, 1995.

Sister Aileen very kindly helped with the compilation of the story of St Michael's Convent.

Page 67 the Gate House Lodges

The two lodges on Ham Common. Evelyn Pritchard, Journal of Richmond Local History Society, no.20, 1999.

Petersham

Pages 68 – 71 the View and Petersham Meadows

The battle for Petersham Meadow. Bernard Marder, Journal of Richmond Local History Society, no.24, 2003.

Letters of César de Saussure. Van Myden (ed), 1902, p.144.

Chris Brasher (1928–2003), the journalist, athlete and businessman, broke the Olympic and British record for the 3000 metre steeplechase in the 1956 Melbourne Olympics, winning Great Britain's first Olympic men's track gold medal since the 1936 Berlin games. He later distinguished himself as a journalist, both with his work for the BBC and his columns for *The Observer*. He was voted British sports journalist of the year in both 1968 and 1976. He also set up a business producing the 'Brasher' lightweight walking boot. His love of the outdoor life led him to organise walks, races and expeditions, as well as the Ranelagh Harriers, his local athletic club in Petersham. His lobbying and fund-raising activities helped to protect parts of Snowdonia from development. In 1981 he organised the first London marathon, and played a dominant part in its later successful development. He was awarded the CBE in 1996. He continued to lobby for the preservation of open spaces and inaugurated the Petersham Trust in 1998.

Pages 74 – 75 Devonshire Lodge/Cottage

Lady Diana Beauclerk (1735–1808), 'Lady Di', was the daughter of the 3rd Duke of Marlborough and lady-in-waiting to Queen Charlotte. She scandalised the aristocratic world by leaving her first husband Viscount Bolingbroke and marrying Topham Beauclerk. She then pursued a career as a talented amateur artist. As well as illustrating and painting portraits she supplied innovative designs to the Wedgwood pottery company.

The Hon. George Lamb was the youngest son of the first Viscount Melbourne. His wife, the Hon. Caroline Lamb, was the daughter of the third Earl of Bessborough. She was buried at St Peter's Church in 1857.

Horace Walpole (1717–97) was one of the leading cultural figures of the 18th century, a writer and collector and a master of the art of letter writing. He was the fourth son of Sir Robert Walpole who was Prime Minister from 1721 to 1742. For a time he was an MP. As well as memoirs of political life and his celebrated Gothic novel *The Castle of Otranto*, he wrote over 3,000 letters spanning 60 years. They are written with wit, intellectual vigour and grace. Often quoted, they provide a lively insight into many of his contemporaries and the manners and tastes of the age. A pioneer of Gothic taste, he settled at Strawberry Hill, an estate of some 40 acres at Twickenham, in 1747. He set about remodelling it with Gothic details, which before his death had made it the most celebrated Gothic house in England. In 1791 he succeeded to the title of the 4th Earl of Orford. His niece Charlotte married Sir Lionel Tollemache, 5th Earl of Dysart.

Mary Berry (1763–1852) and her sister and lifelong companion Agnes came from the North Riding of Yorkshire. Horace Walpole first became acquainted with them in 1787, when he was 70 and they were in their early 20s, and their friendship became both close and affectionate. He described them in a letter to his correspondent the Countess of Ossory in October 1788 as *'the best informed and most perfect creatures I ever saw at their age . . . . entirely natural and unaffected, frank, and being qualified to talk on any subject, nothing is so easy and agreeable as their conversation.'* (from *Letters of Horace Walpole*, Peter Cunningham (ed), as above, vol. ix p.152). The sisters, though not well off, were well-travelled, cultured and educated. When he died in 1797, Walpole left them a house, Little Strawberry Hill near his home in Twickenham, together with a legacy. Mary served as his literary executor, posthumously editing *The Works of Horatio Walpole, Earl of Orford*, published in five volumes by John Murray in 1798.

The Journals and Correspondence of Mary Berry (1763–1852). Lady Theresa Lewis (ed), published in three volumes, Longmans, Green & Co., 1865, vol. III, p.444. Mary's comment was very premature, as she lived to the great age of 89 and was buried in 1852 in the churchyard of St Peter's, along with her sister Agnes who died in the same year at the age of 87.

Pages 76 – 77 The Royal Star and Garter Home and Petersham Common

The Home on the Hill, an exhibition at the Museum of Richmond.

The story of the Royal Star and Garter Home for disabled ex-service men and women, published by them in 2006.

History of Petersham Common. F Nigel Hepper, Journal of Richmond Local History Society, no.28, 2007. He was once a Conservator of the Common and wrote a scientific report on its ecology in 2005/6.

Pages 78 – 83 Old Petersham Lodge

Palaces and Parks of Richmond and Kew. 2 vols., John Cloake, Phillimore & Co., 1995 and 1996.
Vol 1 pages 197–206 and 243–5, and Vol 2 pages 101–4, 119–20, and 190–209 give a detailed history of the house.

Richmond's forgotten house, New Park, Petersham. Nicholas de Salis, *Country Life,* 30 September 1982.

A mansion on a damask cloth. Natalie Rothstein, *Country Life,* 24 June 1965.

The Knyvett Letters 1620–44. Transcribed and edited by Bertram Schofield, Norfolk Record Society, 1949. Another possible connection between the area and the Civil War is Oliver's Mound or Mount in Richmond Park. Although this Mound no longer exists it is clearly marked on the modified plan of New Park by the surveyor E J Eyre, dated 1754, which is reproduced on page 113. The origin of the name is unknown although in November 1647 there is said to have been a large assembly of the Parliamentary army under Lieut.-General Oliver Cromwell at Ham (see *Bygone Richmond.* H M Cundall, page 33).

Old Petersham Lodge, a Royalist refuge after the Civil War. Stephen Pasmore, Journal of Richmond Local History Society, no.4, 1983.

A Handbook of Richmond Park. Coryn de Vere, 1909.

A History of Richmond New Park. 'A Resident', 1877.

History of Richmond New Park. J Lucas, 1877.

Robert Hooke's plans of the Earl of Rochester's house are held at the Surrey Records Office, Woking.

Samuel Molyneux's Letter Book, describing his travels in England between December 1712 and April 1713, includes this account of his visit to New Park. He was an astronomer and at various times MP, one of the lords of Admiralty, and private secretary to the Prince of Wales who later became George II. His Letter Book is in Southampton City Council Records Office.

Tour through the Whole Island of Great Britain. Daniel Defoe, 3 vols, published between 1724 and 1727. The quotation is from vol 1, letter 2, part 3, *Hampshire and Surrey.*

Daniel Defoe (1660–1731) is best known as the author of *Robinson Crusoe,* but he was also famous as a political pamphleteer and is often called the father of modern journalism. The books are innovative partly because Defoe had actually visited the places he described.

In Thomson's poem *Summer* the people referred to are most probably:

1st Earl of <u>Harrington</u>, William Stanhope of Petersham Lodge in New Park
3rd Duke of <u>Queensberry</u>, Charles Douglas (husband of Catherine 'Kitty' Hyde of Douglas House)
Viscount <u>Cornbury,</u> the eldest son of Henry Hyde, 4th Earl of Clarendon. (The Clarendon seat was at Cornbury in Oxfordshire.)

Mrs Jordan's Profession, the story of a great actress and a future king. Claire Tomalin, Viking, 1994.

The fire at New Park, Petersham. Stephen Pasmore, Journal of Richmond Local History Society, no.17, 1996.

A full account of the fire at New Park appeared in the *Weekly Journal or British Gazetteer* for Saturday, 7 October 1721.

Pages 84 – 85 Petersham British School

Petersham British School and the Russell family in Victorian times. George F Bartle, Journal of Richmond Local History Society, no.7, 1986.

Pages 88 – 89 St Peter's Church

Information taken from a lecture on the Church given by John Plant in April 1989. John Plant lived in Petersham for many years and was well known for his voluntary work in the community. He was a historian, local guide, artist, supporter of St. Peter's, committee member and treasurer of a variety of local groups, and died in 2007.

St Peter's Church, survey of churchyard monuments. Roger Bowdler, Historical Analysis and Research Team, English Heritage, August 1999.

History of St Peter's Church. Charles D Warren, Sidgwick & Jackson, 1938. A comprehensive history of the church, including accounts of many of the residents who worshipped there.

Handbook to the Environs of London. James Thorne, 1870, reprinted by Adams & Dart, 1970.

Pages 90 – 111

New light on old Petersham Houses I. John Cloake, Journal of Richmond Local History Society, no.18, 1997. *New light on old Petersham Houses II*. John Cloake, Journal of Richmond Local History Society, no.19, 1998. Both these articles provide authoritative detail of houses in Petersham and their occupants.

Page 90 Petersham House

Country Homes, gardens old and new, Petersham, Surrey and its houses II: Ormeley Lodge and Petersham House. Arthur T Bolton, *Country Life*, 26 October 1918.

Colonel Thomas Panton was a gambler and a rake; he lived in extravagant splendour in lodgings near to Court and made a reputation for himself as a ladies' man. He held commissions in Charles II's army in both the Life and Foot Guards until becoming a Roman Catholic. He married and turned to property speculation, mostly in Piccadilly and the Haymarket, where Panton Street retains his name to the present day. He died in 1685.

Sir Henry Furnese (1658–1712) was knighted in 1691 and appointed to the London Lieutenancy in 1694. Elected to the first directorate of the newly formed Bank of England, he acted as agent for remitting funds to the army. He was created a baronet in 1707 and served as a sheriff of London in 1700–1. He also sat as a Whig MP. His will instructed that a monument be erected on his tombstone to *'God's great goodness to me in advancing me to a considerable estate from a very small beginning'*.

Sir Henry's second marriage was to Matilda, the daughter of Sir Thomas Vernon. Their daughter, who was also called Matilda (1698/9–1721), married in 1715 Richard Edgcumbe (1680–1750), later 1st Baron Edgcumbe. Matilda and Richard's grandson was also called Richard, 2nd Earl of Mount Edgcumbe. He married Lady Sophia (1768–1806), the third daughter of John Hobart, 2nd Earl of Buckinghamshire. The

Edgcumbes lived at Forbes House on Ham Common for about 30 years. Both Richard and his father George held the office of Lord Lieutenant of Cornwall. Richard Edgcumbe was also for a time the Tory MP for Fowey, and an enthusiastic amateur actor and musician. He died at the age of 75 and was buried at St Peter's Church in 1839.

Sir Robert Furnese (1687–1733) inherited the baronetcy from his father Henry and was also a Whig politician.

Nathaniel Halhed (pronounced *Hel-ed*, also sometimes spelt Halhead) was another London merchant. Halhed was buried in 1730 in a family vault at St Peter's Church, where he was later joined by his son William Halhed (1722–86), a director of the Bank of England, and his son Nathaniel Brassey Halhed (1751–1830), a scholar and eminent orientalist.

The 2nd Duchess of Rutland's son Lord Robert Manners sold Petersham House to Bartholomew Burton, the then owner of Montrose House, opposite. He sold it on to Lucy 2nd Duchess of Montrose, Lord Robert's sister, the youngest daughter of the Duchess of Rutland.

In 1850 it became the home of the Walker family. Samuel Walker, a solicitor, is buried in St Peter's churchyard, along with his wife Elizabeth and his sister Ellen, who lived with them. The house was inherited by his only child Rachel Lætetia, who married Henry Lionel Warde. The house was inherited by her son Lionel Warde, and then by his daughter Mrs Marjorie Ashfield.

Pages 90 – 91

The pictures by Thomas R Way (1861–1913), lithographer, were published in *Architectural Remains of Old Richmond, Twickenham, Kew, Petersham and Mortlake*, published by John Lane, 1900, plate XXII B5-22 (Petersham House) and plate XXIII B5-23 (Rutland Lodge).

Thomas R Way, his views in and around Richmond. Patrick Frazer, Journal of Richmond Local History Society, no.24, 2003.

Page 91 Rutland Lodge

Sir John Darnall (1672–1735), a lawyer, was created a serjeant-at-law in 1715 and was knighted in 1724. In the same year he was appointed a judge of the Court of Marshalsea, which administered justice between the king's domestic servants.

Robert Ord (1700–1778). A wealthy man, he was educated at Lincoln's Inn and called to the bar in 1724. He subsequently became an MP for Mitchell in Cornwall but vacated his seat to become chief baron of the Scottish exchequer. Although he was buried in Scotland, his wife Mary was buried with her parents in St Peter's churchyard.

Country Homes, gardens old and new, Petersham, Surrey and its houses III: Rutland Lodge and Douglas House. Arthur T Bolton, *Country Life,* 2 November 1918.

Page 95 Petersham Lodge Woods

The lithograph by William Westall is one of twenty-five views of Richmond which were published between June and August 1822. It was also engraved, along with many others of his, by Joseph Constantine Stadler. The rustic summer house depicted is undoubtedly on the edge of the Woods by the river but is not the Queensberry summer house where John Gay wrote his *Beggar's Opera* (see page 119). Thomas Rowlandson also drew this scene from the other direction.

A view near Richmond. Stephen Pasmore, Journal of Richmond Local History Society, no.6, 1985. This article discusses the Rowlandson painting mentioned above.

The Letters and Journals of Lady Mary Coke. 4 vols, Edinburgh, 1889–96.

Pages 97 – 99 All Saints Church and Village Hall

A gossiping guide to the memorial church of All Saints, Petersham. The Revd W H Oxley, 1910.

Petersham at war: the story of radar training and operational research at All Saints Church. J M Lee, Journal of Richmond Local History Society, no.28, 2007.

All Saints Church, Petersham in wartime. Gillian Hughes, Journal of Richmond Local History Society, no.7, 1986.

Page 99 Reston Lodge

Rebecca Bristow died in 1775 and is buried in the churchyard of St Peter's along with her brother John's

daughter Sophia who died in 1778. One of Sophia's sisters was Caroline, Baroness Westcote who had married, as his second wife, William Henry, 1st Baron Westcote, later 1st Baron Lyttelton (1724–1808). He was a colonial governor and diplomat who also shared some of his brother George Lyttelton's ambitions as a poet and man of letters. He published, privately, a volume entitled *Trifles in Verse* in 1803 and he also wrote the epitaph on his sister-in-law Sophia's tomb in the St Peter's churchyard. The vault also contains the remains of later members of the family, including Ann Catherine Montagu, a married daughter of the Hon. Henry Hobart and his wife Ann Margaret née Bristow, who died in 1808 (see the Hobarts of Ham Common, pages 42–43). Also possibly buried there are the Hon. Mrs Hobart who died in 1788 and another of her daughters, Leonora, who died in 1794.

Pages 100 – 101 Montrose House

Petersham people and stories. The Revd R S Mills, Manor House Press, 1976.

Pages 104 – 105 Village Lock-up and Pound

Most of this information was obtained from John Shorrocks, a police historian from Scotland Yard, who researched the building in the 1990s.

Pages 106 – 107 Beadles/Beating the Bounds

History of St Peter's Church, Petersham. Charles D Warren, Sidgwick and Jackson, 1938 re beadles.

Strange Britain. Information on beating the bounds from the website www.strangebritain.co.uk

Pages 110 – 111 Elm Lodge

Sir Henry Charles Englefield (c.1752–1822), 7th baronet, was an antiquary and science writer who collaborated for a time on optical experiments with Sir Everard Home of the Manor House, Ham. He erected a memorial at St Peter's Church to his aunt, Lady Mary Buck, who lived at Elm Lodge for about 30 years and was a great friend of Lady Diana Beauclerk of Devonshire Lodge.

William Robert Spencer (1770–1834) was a poet and humorist, and grandson of the 3rd Duke of Marlborough. His wit and accomplishments made him very popular in London society. He married Susan, the widow of Count Spreti, in 1791 and they had five sons and two daughters. He became a commissioner of stamps from 1797 to 1826 but owing to financial difficulties had to leave Petersham in 1825 to live in Paris. He died in a state of poverty and ill health in 1834.

Charles Dickens at Petersham. Margaret Evans, Journal of Richmond Local History Society, no.15, 1994.

Charles Dickens sings the praises of Petersham in a letter dated 28 June 1839 to his close friend the painter Daniel Maclise (1806–70). In the same year Maclise was commissioned by the publishers Chapman and Hall to paint the portrait of Dickens which now hangs in the National Portrait Gallery. His talent and charm won Maclise many patrons and friends in the intellectual and literary world.

Life of Charles Dickens. John Forster, Cecil Palmer, London, 1872–4, reprinted Dent, 1969, Book II: *During and after 'Nickleby',* 1838 and 1839. Forster is referring to the summer of 1839. 'The Petersham races' probably refers to the races held every summer at that time on Ham Common. 'Mr Beard' was Thomas Beard, a journalist friend.

Woodbine Cottage, Petersham. John Beardmore and Dr David Parker, Journal of Richmond Local History Society, no.20, 1999.

Daisy Ashford – her life. R M Malcomson, Chatto & Windus, the Hogarth Press, 1984.

Pages 112 – 117 Sudbrook Park

Sudbrook and its occupants. H M Cundall, Adam and Charles Black, 1912.

Two dukes and their houses. Mary Cosh, *Country Life,* 13 July 1972.

Country homes, gardens old and new, Petersham, Surrey and its houses I: Sudbrook Park. Arthur T Bolton, *Country Life,* 19 October 1918.

Some Account of John, Duke of Argyll and his Family. Lady Louisa Stuart, privately published in 1863 for Caroline Lucy, Lady Scott.

Letters of Horace Walpole, Peter Cunningham (ed), as above. The letter referring to Charles Townshend's marriage is from 1755 vol. ii p.450.

Lady Mary Coke and her journal 1726–1811. Stephen Pasmore, Journal of Richmond Local History Society, no.7, 1986.

The Letters and Journals of Lady Mary Coke. 4 vols, Edinburgh, 1889–96.

Page 118 van Gogh and the Wesleyan Methodist chapel

Vincent van Gogh in Richmond and Petersham. Stephen Pasmore, Journal of Richmond Local History Society, no.1, 1981.

Pages 119 – 121 Douglas House

Country Homes, gardens old and new, Petersham, Surrey and its houses III: Rutland Lodge and Douglas House. Arthur T Bolton, *Country Life,* 2 November 1918.

Walpole's reference to the death of the Duchess of Queensberry is from *Letters of Horace Walpole,* Peter Cunningham (ed), as above, vol.vi p.461.

Frances, Lady Douglas (1750–1817) was the subject of a memoire written by Lady Louisa Stuart (1757–1851), youngest daughter of the 3rd Earl of Bute, for Frances's daughter Caroline Lucy Scott (1784–1857). (*Memoire of Frances, Lady Douglas,* J Rubenstein (ed), Scottish Academic Press, 1985).

A drawing by John Constable,
RA *A woman by an old
Willow Tree at Ham, Surrey*
(see notes on page 126/127)
©*V&A Images/Victoria and
Albert Museum, London*

Index